P9-CNC-276

WE BRAKE FOR JOY!

WE BRAKE FOR JOY!

90 Devotions to Add Laughter, Fun, and Faith to Your Life

PATSY CLAIRMONT BARBARA JOHNSON
MARILYN MEBERG LUCI SWINDOLL
SHEILA WALSH THELMA WELLS

with JANET KOBOBEL GRANT

ZondervanPublishingHouse
Grand Rapids, Michigan
A Division of HarperCollins*Publishers*

We Brake for Joy!

Requests for information should be addressed to:
ZondervanPublishingHouse
Grand Rapids, Michigan 49530

Library of Congress Cataloging-in-Publication Data

We brake for joy : 90 devotions to add laughter, fun, and faith to your life / Patsy Clairmont . . . [et al.].
p. cm.
ISBN: 0-310-22042-4
1. Christian women—Prayer-books and devotions—English. I. Clairmont, Patsy.
BV4844.W4 1998
242'.643-dc 21 98-17614
CIP

For any copyrighted material, every effort has been made to contact the copyright holders for permission. If any copyright holder feels that he or she has been overlooked, please contact the author care of the publisher, and appropriate measures will be taken.

Scripture quotations are from:

The Holy Bible, New International Version (NIV), © 1973, 1984 by the International Bible Society. Used by permission of Zondervan Publishing House;

New American Standard Bible (NASB), © 1960, 1977 by the Lockman Foundation;

The New King James Version (NKJV), © 1984 by Thomas Nelson, Inc.;

The Living Bible (TLB), © 1971 by Tyndale House Publishers.

This edition printed on acid-free paper and meets the American National Standards Institute Z39.48 standard.

Printed in the United States of America

98 99 00 01 02 03 04 /❖ DC/ 10 9 8 7 6 5 4 3 2 1

CONTENTS

Part Five

Wide Load (I Beg Your Pardon!): *Stuff We Get to, Want to, Have to Lug Through Life*

Part Six
Fill 'er Up: *Refueling Your Soul*

HONK IF YOU GIGGLED TODAY

Developing a Mirthful Mind-set

DWAYNE'S DAY

Luci Swindoll

One man considers one day more sacred than another; another man considers every day alike. Each one should be fully convinced in his own mind. He who regards one day as special, does so to the Lord.

ROMANS 14:5–6

An edict went out from the Board to offer an additional holiday to all Mobil employees. This was like a breath of fresh air around the laboratory where I worked. We were thrilled. Forms were sent out for everyone to submit his or her day of preference.

My friend Doris, a secretary, asked her boss his request. Dwayne was a rather unconventional but highly intelligent Ph.D.

"August 12," Dwayne said.

"August 12? Are you sure?"

"Well . . . yeah. Why do you ask? Have a lot of people requested that day?"

"No. No one. I guess I wonder why you do."

"Because it's a Friday. I like Fridays off."

"But next year it won't be Friday."

"Oh, that's right. . . . Well, what have most people requested?"

"Most people want the day after Thanksgiving."

"But I already take that Friday as a day of vacation."

A bit exasperated, Doris tried to calmly state the obvious. "Dwayne, if the company gives you the day off, you wouldn't *have* to take it as a vacation day. It would already *be* a holiday. You'd have a long weekend . . . you know, four days together."

With all the seriousness in the world, Dwayne shot back, "Then what day would I take as a day of vacation?"

Giving up, Doris replied, "How 'bout August 12?"

That settled it for Dwayne. "Great idea."

Doris shook her head and walked away.

I've laughed at this story for years. Dear, sweet Dwayne, brilliant but baffled by such simple things. Every August 12 I think of him. I do something different that day . . . phone one of my old pals from the laboratory in Dallas and chat . . . bake a batch of muffins in Dwayne's honor . . . look through photos from the sixties, and remember my friends from the Mobil lab.

I like having special days set aside to commemorate an event: birthdays, anniversaries, graduations. My journals are full of remembrances like "Forty years ago today my parents were married." Or "Six years ago I broke my leg." Or "If my father had lived, he'd be ninety today." Or, "Remember, Luci, three years ago you bought this house."

Days are important. I anticipate them. I'm looking forward to the day my friends come for Thanksgiving, to the next time I'll see my brother in Florida. And I can never quite wait for Christmas.

The word *days* appears more than five hundred times in Scripture, and the Mosaic Law prescribed feast days when the congregation was to celebrate by dancing, singing, resting from labor, and giving praise to God. These were occasions of joy and gladness.

I encourage you to create special days for yourself and your family. Twenty-four hours when you do something entirely different from other days . . . or maybe do nothing. Barbara Johnson declares the first day of each month a holiday. She reserves it just *for herself*. She calls me and says, "Take a bath and change your sheets. It's the first day of the month!" These twelve days are singular and individual to Barbara. I love that!

The happiest people I know are those who are fully convinced in their own minds that *this* is the day the Lord has made. They rejoice and are glad in it. Celebrate *all* your days—including August 12.

"Give us joy this day, Lord, in knowing you. And help us remember that every day we are alive is your gift to us. Amen."

A GIFT FROM THE SCRAP PILE

Barbara Johnson

So take a new grip with your tired hands, stand firm on your shaky legs, and mark out a straight, smooth path for your feet so that those who follow you, though weak and lame, will not fall and hurt themselves, but become strong.

HEBREWS 12:12–13 TLB

Charles Darrow was out of work and as poor as a pauper during the Depression, but he kept a smile on his face and a sparkle in his eye. He didn't want his wife, expecting their first child, to be discouraged; so every night when he returned to their little apartment after standing in the unemployment lines all day, he would tell her funny stories about the things he had seen—or imagined.

Darrow was a clever man, and he was always coming up with notions that made people laugh. (He wasn't at all like the lady who said she once had a bright idea—but it died of loneliness.)

Darrow knew how powerfully his own attitude affected his wife. His temperament was the color his wife used to paint her own mood. If he came home weary and irritable, her spirits fell, and her smile vanished. On the other hand, if she heard him whistling a merry tune as he climbed the many flights of stairs up to their tiny rooms, she would fling open the door and scamper out to the railing to lean over and smile at him as he wound his way up the staircase. They fed on the gift of each other's joy.

In his younger years, Darrow had enjoyed happy family vacations in nearby Atlantic City, and he drew on those memories to keep his spirits high. He developed a little game on a square piece of cardboard. Around the edges he drew a series of "properties" named after the streets and familiar places he had visited during those pleasant childhood summers. He carved little houses and hotels out of scraps of wood, and as he and his young wife played the game each evening, they pretended to be rich, buying and selling property and "building" homes and hotels like extravagant tycoons. On those long, dark evenings, that impoverished apartment was filled with the sound of laughter.

Charles Darrow didn't set out to become a millionaire when he developed "Monopoly," the game that was later marketed around the world by Parker Brothers, but that's what happened. The little gift he developed from scraps of cardboard and tiny pieces of wood was simply a way to keep his wife's spirits up during her Depression-era pregnancy; ultimately, that gift came back to him as bountiful riches.

Monopoly is still being sold by the thousands more than fifty years later. Every time I think of those little green houses and red hotels, the unusual game pieces, and those "get out of jail" cards that made us all race around the game board with gleeful abandon, I see an example of shared joy. Darrow created a gift of joy, shared it with the world, and the gift came right back to him a thousand-fold.

Are times tough in your little apartment—or lavish mansion? Are you weary from standing in lines that lead to nowhere? If it seems as if your world is collapsing around you and you feel yourself slipping down into the depths of depression, don't despair. As someone said, "Even the sun sinks every night—but it rises again every morning." Remember that the right temperature in a home is maintained by warm hearts, not by icy glares, lukewarm enthusiasm—or hotheads! Your attitude can set the tone for your whole family. So use whatever scraps you can find—even if, in the beginning, it's just a scrap of a smile—and make a gift of whatever you have. Then watch the gifts come back to you.

"Dear Lord, when times are tough, please help me see that your gifts of love and grace are always there for me. Show me how I can pull together the scraps of my life, tie them up with your love, and share that gift with others. Amen."

HOW'S THE WEATHER?

Marilyn Meberg

He turned the desert into pools of water
and the parched ground into flowing springs.

PSALM 107:35

Palm Desert, California, where I live, is for eight and sometimes nine months of the year a paradise. I bask in daily sunshine under blue skies with winter temperatures in the seventies.

Since I am "solar-powered," the presence of the sun is crucial to my sense of well-being. Growing up in the Pacific Northwest, where even summer picnics were frequently rained out, I was thrilled when, in 1961, Ken and I married and headed south for Garden Grove, California.

Ken grew up in Seattle and was far more drizzle-driven than solar-powered. As a result, our first couple of years in the sunny Southland were a bit of a challenge for him. He was surprised to find he missed the gray, sloppy days to which he had become accustomed. (Mark Twain said the mildest winter he ever experienced was the summer he spent in Seattle.)

Even though I, too, grew up in the Northwest, I never got used to what felt like year-round winter. I didn't realize how much I was oppressed by rain until we moved to Southern California, but my spirits soared the minute we landed in the Los Angeles basin. I'm kind of embarrassed to have my mental health so strongly influenced by the absence of rain and the presence of sun, but it seems to be a fact, whether I'm proud of it or not.

To celebrate our first wedding anniversary, Ken suggested we go to Palm Springs. It was only two hours away, and the hotel rates were reduced because it was the third week of June. Neither of us knew much about Palm Springs except that it sounded like a wonderfully exotic and romantic place to go. That it was located in the Mojave desert didn't strike us as a problem.

As we pulled up to our charming bungalow motel, we noticed the temperature sign on the bank across the street read 117 degrees. That was a bit shocking; we had heard about that kind of temperature but certainly never experienced it.

"This is absurd," Ken snorted, dropping our bags in the middle of the room and falling onto the bed. "Who in his right mind lives in a place like this? Who in his right mind pays to visit a place like this? The air's even too hot to breathe! I'm surprised the streets and sidewalks aren't littered with dead people suffocated by this air!"

"Maybe the city carts off the bodies before they accumulate," I suggested. Since that thought didn't seem to strike Ken as clever, I suggested we stand in the deep end of the pool and breathe through a reed until the sun went down. Making another stab at being clever I said, "Maybe being surrounded by all that water will remind you of Seattle." This time he chuckled and said he would beat me into the pool.

Within a few minutes, we tamed our environment and had a fabulous time. Since we were the only ones in the pool (the others had probably been carted off by the city before we arrived), I sat lipline in the water while Ken took flying leaps off the diving board. I flashed numerical ratings with my fingers and, with shouts of encouragement, told him his dives were rapidly working their way to a perfect ten.

That night we splurged and had a romantic dinner at the Riviera Country Club, played the next day in our still-vacated pool, and then headed home.

"Ken," I sighed contentedly. "I think I've fallen in love with the desert. I'd love to live there some day."

"Are you kidding? That's like saying you'd like to live in an ashtray. No way!"

Ironically, some twenty-three years later, Ken became superintendent of the Desert Sands School District, which encompasses those communities from the city limits of Palm Springs through the city of Indio. An even greater irony is that Ken came to love the desert so much he preferred it to the beach. So, too, do I, although it took *me* only twenty minutes to decide.

One of the things I find fascinating about God's creation is the way he seems to temper the negative environmental elements with corresponding positive ones. For instance, without the nearly ceaseless rains of the Northwest, no incomparable green scenery would greet the eye from all directions. And the snow that snuggles over Mt. Hood, Mt. Rainier, and Mt. St. Helens would not exist if, at lower elevations, there were no rain. Imprinted forever in my sensory memory is the pungent smell of the rich, damp soil that suggests a mixture of pine needles, grass, and moss. I grew up with that scent in my nostrils, and even today, it's one of my favorite smells.

By the same token, if God had not created water for the desert environment, it would indeed be an ashtray. But because of water, we have luxuriously green golf courses, languidly swaying palm trees, and even streams in the desert. Ringing all this valley lushness is the beauty of the San Jacinto Mountains, which turn into a kaleidoscope of pinks, blues, and lavenders each evening as the sun sets.

God's creative style ensures that something wonderful will offset something less than wonderful. In everything God seems so balanced. I love that about him. I also love that he has placed me in the desert where, during June, July, and August, I can be found either at the deep end of the pool breathing through a reed or at the top of a mountain reading a book.

"Lord Jesus, thank you that you have indeed given abundant life to us your children. Thank you for the richness and beauty of that life. Grant to me always the will to see that beauty and the spirit to see it as a gift from your loving hand. Amen."

STAR STRUCK

Patsy Clairmont

He also made the stars.

Genesis 1:16

I felt like Michelangelo himself, as I swayed back and forth on my ladder creating a masterpiece. While, I confess, the ceiling I was working on wasn't as lofty as the Sistine Chapel, it was high enough for me, thank you. And I wasn't painting the hand of God; no, it was more like the handiwork of God.

You see, I was pressing the heavenlies into place on my then-young son Jason's bedroom ceiling—luminous stars, hundreds of them, along with planets, and a few comets for flare. One by one I secured them, taking time to scatter some about the perimeter for visual effect. Finally, after the addition of Mars and Pluto, I was done. I then waited for nightfall and the suspenseful unveiling.

When evening overtook our land, I steered Jason, who was blindfolded, up the stairs to his room. (I'm into drama.) Then, *voila!* I uncovered his eyes, and to my delight (and his longevity), he was pleased. He made all the right sounds. *Oohs* and *ahs* abounded as I pointed to the different parts of the "sky."

I guess I'm like most parents in that I would give my children the world if I could. We feel the sky is the limit for those we love. And isn't it marvelous that we, too, have a Parent who offers us all that we will ever need? He who hung the sun, the moon, and the stars, surveyed his efforts, and said, (*Voila!*) "It is good," was pleased to design the universe's wonders and then to present them to us. Imagine that.

I wonder what exclamation escaped Adam when he saw his first rhino, baboon, and ostrich. I bet if he had had a horn, he would have honked it that day. Or think of the series of *oohs* sung by Eve (which was probably the first aria) when she experienced a crimson sunset. And imagine the magnificent view the first couple must have had of the firmament without the distraction and diffusion of city lights and pollution.

Scripture tells us, "Every good and perfect gift is from above, coming down from the Father of the heavenly lights, who does not change like shifting shadows" (James 1:17). Our God is a gift giver. His generosity is obvious in how lavishly he bestows on us rainbows, waterfalls, canyons, and white caps. Few things are as soul-stirring for me as the designs in creation. They cause me to take time out of my busy life to literally brake for joy—visual joy!

As a matter of fact, one day when I was visiting in the desert, a marshmallow cloud formation drizzled over the mountaintop like so much whipped cream. I brought my bike to a standstill and just beheld this delicious scene for thirty-five minutes. Another evening the sunset turned the skyline into a saucer of peaches and cream—absolutely dreamy. The Lord serves up his scrumptious beauty in liberal portions and then invites us to partake. His *voilas* turn into wonderment for me.

From Marilyn's (Meberg, who else?) patio, she and her guests can view a ring of mountains. I have often joined her at nightfall for the spectacular performance as the sun sets. The mountains go through a series of thrilling changes. From pinks to lavenders to deep purples, the setting sun and emerging evening appear to cover the hillside for sleep. Marilyn and I never tire of the Lord's thrilling displays. We *ooh* and *ah* in all the right places, and we can feel our blood pressure balancing out as smiles and giggles of pleasure help us to express our gratitude. And we, like Adam, would honk if we had a horn.

"Lord, in a world so often dark with sin, thank you for the light from your creation that continues to fill our lives with smiles, giggles, gratitude, and hope. Amen."

THE ONE WITH THE WHITE LEGS

Sheila Walsh

The LORD appeared to us in the past, saying:
"I have loved you with an everlasting love;
I have drawn you with loving-kindness."

JEREMIAH 31:3

God's love is a gift that can make you forget yourself at times, just like Uncle Hugh did on a cold winter's day when I was twelve years old.

We tumbled in out of the cold winter air and the wind that whipped our hair against our faces. I loved the warm fire and familiar smells of my Nana's house. Every Sunday after the morning service at Ayr Baptist Church, Stephen, Frances, and I went to Nana's for lunch so we could make it back in time for Sunday school at three o'clock.

This Sunday was special, however. The whole family was there as well as a favorite aunt and uncle. They weren't actually family, but we had called them that since we were children, and we loved them. My aunt had brought her father, too, whom we called Uncle Hugh.

Uncle Hugh was a fascinating character. His face had stories written all over it that he kept to himself. He sat by the fire and refused to come to the table with the rest of us, so he was served where it was warm and cozy. My brother, sister, and I noted that when you're old you're given fireside eating privileges.

Uncle Pete was just about to give thanks when Uncle Hugh turned on the television. My aunt was mortified. Not only was it Sunday, when watching television was frowned upon, but also her dad had turned on horse racing!

"Dad, put that off this minute!" she cried.

"I will not!" he shouted over his soup. "This is a big race."

I sat captivated by this adult confrontation. *Who wins when everyone is big?* I wondered.

My grandmother was a kind and peaceable soul, and she managed to negotiate a compromise. Uncle Hugh could watch the race if he turned off the sound. With this treaty signed, Uncle Pete launched into a lengthy grace fit for a Sunday. Halfway through his prayer of thanksgiving, a voice from across the room bellowed, "Man, would you look at that one with the white legs!"

For a moment no one dared to breathe. Then my mother lost all composure and almost fell off her chair with laughter. We all laughed. We laughed until the tears rolled off our cheeks.

Just as the Scottish writer George MacDonald said, "It is the heart that is not yet sure of its God that is afraid to laugh in his presence."

So often with old people and children all sense of what would be appropriate is swallowed up in what feels right. That's refreshing. We waste too many years between childhood and our older years measuring our behavior on a scale we think we see in someone else's eyes.

God loves us as we are right now! That's one of the things I'm most grateful for. I love the freedom to be myself in God. I pray that a year from now, five years from now, I will be a more godly woman, but I know God won't love me any more than he does right this minute.

Do you find yourself coming into God's presence carefully, wondering what kind of reception you'll get? Let me tell you, you can run in out of the cold, sit by the fire, put up your feet, and just be yourself. You are loved, you are loved, you are loved . . . even with white legs!

"Lord, thank you for loving me with an everlasting love. Help me today to live in that love and share that love with others. Amen."

SAYING THE THREE WORDS

Thelma Wells

But the greatest of these is love.

I CORINTHIANS 13:13

For the first eighteen years of my married life, I wanted my husband to say three specific words. Maybe he had said them once or twice but, apparently, so seldom I couldn't recall hearing them.

I would say, "Please, baby, just tell me you love me. Even if you're lying, just say it!"

He would respond, "Why do I have to say *that?* You know I do. It don't make sense to have to say *that* when I show you all the time."

Then I'd beg, "I know you show me, and I appreciate that. But just say it. It won't hurt."

Do I have to tell you that nothing ever came of those conversations?

Now, my husband's background is different from mine. His father had thirty-one sisters and brothers. That's what I said, thirty-one. I have the names and birthdays all recorded to prove it.

They grew up on a huge farm in south Texas where they raised everything they ate. They had cattle, pigs, chickens, sugar cane, vegetables, wheat (and their own flour mill), cotton, fishing tank, and—God forbid—homemade whiskey. The kids worked all the time when they weren't in school. The family lived in a seven-room home in which the bedrooms were nearly as large as some houses. The boys slept in two rooms, and the girls slept in two rooms.

I suppose they were together so much that the words "I love you" never occurred to them to say. At least, not to the boys. They were taught to be men, and men didn't show emotion. Men didn't cry. Men didn't say mushy stuff. That's the environment my husband was raised in.

Me, I'm a city slicker from Dallas. No horses, cows, and pigs for me. The closest I came to a farm was Granny's yard where she planted a patch of greens and beans. Concord grapes grew on the fence, and one year a couple of watermelons showed up in the garden. Three of us lived in our house. We had one bedroom, a sleep sofa, and a rollaway bed on the screened-in front porch. But something was practiced in our house that I will forever appreciate. We often used the words "I love you."

So when I married George, we wrangled over those words and getting him to say them. Years later we hosted our eighteen-year-old daughter's debutante reception. During her presentation she had great things to say about her parents. But one story she told captured the hearts of the two hundred people attending.

"Ever since I was a little girl," Vikki started out, "my mama would tell us she loves us. My father would never tell us. I would say, 'Daddy, I love you,' and he would always say, 'I know it, Vikki.'

"Well, Daddy, I finally figured out what you mean when you say, 'I know it, Vikki.' You're really saying, 'I love you, too.' So Daddy, it's all right. Keep on saying what you say, and I'll know what you mean."

That story set everyone off. Some people were sniffing and crying. Some had wet eyes that they tried to dab at when no one was looking. Even my macho husband was crying. Mr. Non-Emotional, Won't-Speak-in-Public-Before-a-Large-Group meandered to the microphone and said, "Come here, Vikki, Daddy wants to tell you something." Holding the microphone in one hand and putting his arm around Vikki, he said, "Daddy loves you, Vikki. Daddy's proud of you."

Almost every week since that monumental day in 1981 he's been telling us he loves us. Hallelujah!

Do you enjoy hearing those tender words from your spouse, children, family, and friends? Of course you do. However, to know that we are loved by an omnipotent, omnipresent, omniscient Lord is the grandest feeling of acceptance anyone can have. When other people fail to express their love to us, we can always depend on Jesus.

Imagine Jesus himself saying to you, "Child of mine, I love you with an everlasting love. I love you with unconditional love. I love you because I want to! I love you when others think you are unlovable. I love you when you have sinned and come short of my glory. I love you in the good times and in the bad."

"God, we can't comprehend the depth of your love. We do know that without your loving protection we would be in danger. Without your loving provision we would be in want. Without your loving correction we would remain rebellious. Without your loving care we wouldn't know compassion. Without your loving Son we wouldn't be saved. When we begin to attach strings to our love for someone, even by demanding they tell us they love us, remind us that you have no strings attached to your love. Amen."

MONDAY MUSINGS

Luci Swindoll

Whatever you do, work at it with all your heart, as working for the Lord, not for men, since you know that you will receive an inheritance from the Lord as a reward. It is the Lord Christ you are serving.

COLOSSIANS 3:23–24

Mondays ... too many chores. Since I travel most weekends, Monday is the day I unpack. That's always a mess, with stuff strewn everywhere and suitcases lying about. Being a neat-nick, I hate that.

Then there's the laundry ... piles of clothes that need washing. And those piles multiply in the night! I have this theory that, after the Lord comes and time is no more, somewhere, in a corner of the world, dirty laundry will still be waiting, multiplying.

On Monday I must make stops at the grocery store, the cleaners, the bank, the post office, the service station, the hairdresser ... Deliver me! Mondays annoy me.

But ... not completely. In another way, I love Mondays. I love unloading all my stuff out of the suitcase and organizing it back where it belongs. That satisfies me. I love pulling fresh laundry from the dryer and folding it while it's still warm.

And, frankly, I've grown to love the bank. Why, I have my own teller. Her name is Gwen. She's a sweetheart with a ready smile and a warm heart. She's a Christian who's helpful and patient. I give her books my brother has written. She loves that, and I experience such joy in making her happy. We have great chats.

And, you know, I also love grocery shopping. I love having all those choices and anticipating the preparation of wonderful meals. I grab up fresh bouquets of flowers and never quite seem to get the smile off my face. Every now and then, I add a jar of pickles, can of hairspray, or package of liverwurst to another shopper's unattended cart, just to entertain myself and give that person whiplash at the checkout counter.

Even the post office can be rewarding. I love buying stamps. Last week, I bought ten stamps and gave two each to the five people behind me. I told them I hated waiting in line and was sure they did, too. But, for doing so, I was giving them a little present. My own little random act of kindness.

On Monday nights, I feel genuine joy, having such a sense of accomplishment. Plus, I've had a few good laughs, enjoyed a meaningful chat or two, and expressed love in a tangible way to total strangers.

So what's the difference? Why do I sometimes get bogged down with chores, hating the day? Then, at other times, I get fired up with enthusiasm, loving the day? Perspective! Perspective is everything. Paul encourages us to do whatever we do with all our hearts. He tells us to put our soul into it. Like the old song says, "You gotta have heart." When you do, you can do anything. The busiest days can become our most joyful.

We all have things in life we have to do, but we can choose how we want to do them. It's up to each of us. I can tell you this, though. There's only one way to have joy . . . by doing everything "as unto the Lord."

By the way, if you're the one who arrived at home with an extra jar of pickles, enjoy them. Toss them in a salad and look at it this way: You helped bring a smile to someone today. Perspective is everything.

"Help us realize, Father, that life is what we make it. Teach us to make it new every morning . . . fun, fresh, and fulfilling. We thank you that you care about every day of our lives—even Mondays! Amen."

AN UNUSUAL SONG

Marilyn Meberg

Sing joyfully to the LORD.

PSALM 33:1

Prior to a month ago, if anyone had asked if I had an opinion about rain gutters, I would have stared blankly. I have strong political opinions, theological opinions, and even social opinions, but no gutter opinions.

For instance, I have a strong opinion about the color chartreuse. It should be outlawed. Anyone caught wearing it, sitting on it, or using it in any way should be fined heavily and then forced to develop a pleasant working relationship with my computer. Because of the perverse nature of my computer, the latter punishment will prove to be a life sentence.

But an opinion about rain gutters? Well, all that has changed. My conversion experience took place about a month ago.

It began with the warnings about the coming El Niño storms this winter. Since I live in the desert, torrential rains are rare experiences for us. However, given the crabby as well as capricious nature of El Niño, I began to wonder if my little condo shouldn't have rain gutters. The one rain we had last winter did provide a bit of an exit challenge, since the water from the roof above the doorways had nowhere to go but straight down my collar and into my shoes.

When the yellow-page gutter man appeared at my door and asked, "Where do you want your gutters?" I was taken aback. I had assumed the fellow would thread gutters around the roofline of my condo and go home.

"Well," I said falteringly, "I don't want to be rain battered when I come out the door so I guess I want the gutters to prevent that . . . "

"So you want them over your two doors?"

I began to realize how greatly I had underestimated the varietal potential of gutters. In a matter of minutes the two of us decided on a custom design that would accommodate my particular ground slope, door positions, and garage location. Never in my life had I considered the various means by which one could divert water down little pipes and spouts that would ultimately spill out somewhere other than down my clothing.

I became so fascinated with the placement of gutters, I couldn't ride bikes with Luci and Patsy without veering off course to sidle up to someone's wall and inspect their gutter configuration. I discovered gutters could dump into shrubbery outside the patio, be positioned with a graceful curve to dump onto the driveway, or even into a neighbor's living room! The potential is limitless.

One configuration on a condo two streets from me greatly troubles me. I don't see how it can work efficiently because, as I peered over the five-foot wall into their back patio, it appeared to me the gutter water wouldn't exit far enough from the slider door. I fear when El Niño comes blustering into our town, these people will have a flooded bedroom.

I would express my concern to them, but they never seem to be home. However, last week I noticed through their dining room window a slightly chartreuse dry-flower arrangement on their coffee table. I've decided I won't make any further efforts to advise them.

All this gutter business highlights a basic tenet for joyful living: the little things in life tend to absorb me, please me, or give me a giggle. I had no idea a world of rain-gutter information was out there waiting to be discovered. But now that I've found it, the subject has provided great pleasure for me.

I must admit, though, the audience for my newfound knowledge seems limited. When Luci, Patsy, and I go bike riding, and I dash off for an inspection along the way, they increase their pedal efforts and disappear around a corner. Neither of them seems to have any desire to develop an opinion about rain gutters. But I guess that's okay. At least their bikes are the right color.

"Lord, I love that you are the source of all joy, the inspiration for all song. Thank you that you inspire joyful singing in not only the usual places but also in the unusual. Thank you for new things to sing about and new things to know about. Amen."

PACIFIED

Patsy Clairmont

When I was a child . . .

1 CORINTHIANS 13:11

Recently, I had the most mirthful thought; it came to me during church. A man rose during the service and walked up the aisle toward the back carrying his young child. The toddler obviously was not impressed with the sermon. To keep everyone from knowing the extent of the child's displeasure, the father had corked him. A pacifier protruded from the little one's mouth keeping his fussiness firmly bottled. His face appeared a tad red from holding in his opinions, but the pacifier did seem to accomplish its purpose.

Now, here's my thought: I'd like to manufacture adult pacifiers. What do you think? It makes me want to honk and giggle. Too outrageous, you say? Well, not so quick.

Don't you know some pretty fussy people that you'd like to . . . cork? C'mon now, be honest. Why, those rubber stoppers might prevent unnecessary dissension, promote goodwill among humankind, and even breed greater contentment. Are you catching the vision?

I can recall a number of times I should have taken a couple of good swigs on a pacifier instead of a couple of verbal swings at an antagonizer. We would all have been better off if I had. My joy certainly would have increased, for I have found my first words are not always my finest choices. Instead, my reactive whirl of words has the capacity to be outlandish. More often than I'd like to admit, my verbal response is based in an unsteady emotion such as hurt. (And hurt can be as fickle as love.) In my attempt to hide my hurt and protect my vulnerable (and prideful) heart, I have used lashing language that puts others *en garde*. My reaction conveys an inaccurate message. It shouts, "I'm angry" rather than confessing, "I'm hurt."

Also, the sharp edge of lashing language can wound the recipient. In the heat of the moment, that's somewhat satisfying. *Touché!* Yet, when our feelings cool and our brains settle down, we almost always regret our knee-jerk (emphasis on *jerk*) reaction.

That's where the pacifiers fit in. Imagine how differently events would have unfolded if pacifiers had been applied appropriately. For example, picture Peter in the Garden of Gethsemane. Instead of whipping out his sword to whack off the soldier's ear, Peter would have raised his hand indicating a five-minute time-out. Then he'd reach for a small leather sack tied to his waist and pull out a well-worn pacifier. After several reflective pulls on his binkie, he would realize how inappropriate lashing out would be and instead turn to the Lord for direction.

See, this idea has merit. In fact, I can envision these teensy comforters being installed as standard equipment on automobiles. Honk, honk. Then, when the guy on the highway gets in our way, we push a button (instead of laying on the horn) which, in turn, releases our binkie from above our heads. We grab onto our pacifier and, after several deep slurps, feel prepared to continue on our journey more . . . well, pacified.

And what about school? Don't you think every high school should attach binkies to the desks? Then, when belligerence is the 'tude of the moment, teachers and students alike could unwind during a binkie break. Or maybe they could have a binkie room or a pacifier parlor instead of a detention hall. That way the rebellious could ruminate rather than rumble.

I'd manufacture different colored pacifiers to go with our outfits, moods, and decor. I'd give the mouthpieces as gifts, tons of them. I'd offer them personalized, iridescent, flavored, and gold-trimmed. I'd organize pacifier conventions and even have marathons to reward the person who stays plugged the longest.

Only one thing niggles at me about this idea. It's the rest of our opening verse, "I put childish ways behind me." Oh, phooey, that kinda spoils my frivolity.

How about you? Playing any childish games? Need to grow up?

"Lord, help me not to look for an easy way out like a child seeking recess or a toddler searching for her pacifier. Help me to take responsibility before you and others for my actions and reactions. Thank you that I can choose to give up my childishness and instead experience childlike joy. Amen."

JOY COMETH IN THE MAILBAG

Barbara Johnson

Do not grieve, for the joy of the LORD is your strength.

NEHEMIAH 8:10

Bill and I travel to speaking engagements as many as thirty-nine weekends a year, and sometimes we find ourselves standing in the carport on Sunday afternoons almost too exhausted to unload the luggage.

But as soon as I walk in the door, one of the first things that catches my eye is the huge stack of mail a neighbor has collected for us and left on the kitchen table. In one of my recent books, *Joy Journal*, the publisher included little postcards at the end that readers could tear out and mail to me. As I'm standing there, wondering how I'll summon the energy to unpack our bags and catch up on all the work, inevitably I pick up a piece of mail, perhaps one of those little postcards, and read it. Here's a sample of one recent batch of postcards:

> Barbara, Because you were not accusing and judging of us, it has helped us not to accuse or judge our son—just keep loving him and keep our communication going between him and us and between the Lord and us. May his love through you and through us bring healing.

> Dear Barbara, Do not be afraid of tomorrow.... God is already there.

> Dear Barbara, You are wonderful! May God richly bless you as you have blessed me.

Dear Barbara, Truly God has blessed you to help all us ladies with so much laughter! Keep the joy coming!

Dear Barbara, It's true—of all the things I've lost, I miss my mind the most. It's hard to be nostalgic when you can't remember anything! I've always tried to keep an open mind—and as a result, while I wasn't looking, everything I ever knew flew out the door!

Dear Barbara, Have you heard this one? "Not everyone can be a star. Some of us are just black holes!"

Standing there reading the mail, my batteries are quickly recharged with joy, and pretty soon I'm scurrying around our home with a smile on my face and a song in my heart. (It also helps that while I'm stalling in the kitchen, Bill is lugging the luggage into the bedroom and unpacking it!) Proverbs 17:22 says, "A cheerful heart is good medicine," and that's the tonic I receive when I read these uplifting messages. Suddenly my small kitchen shares something in common with God's glorious heaven, where, according to 1 Chronicles 16:27, "Strength and joy [are] in his dwelling place."

After the complicated work of writing another book or an exhausting trip for an extended speaking engagement, I sometimes feel as if I've given all I can. Whatever project it is, I fling it out to the world . . . and then it comes back to me, bearing strength and joy in the words of women (and men, too) from all over the globe.

Of course, my mail includes letters filled with hurt and pain, too—the heartfelt cries of parents who have lost a child through death or alienation. But the joyful letters give me the strength to encourage those parents as I realize that many of them once wrote to me with the same devastating heartache as the "new" parents are expressing. And now, here they are, able to smile once more and even share a little laughter. They have seen God turn their grief into joy—and that has become their strength. Who do you know who could use an uplifting word today?

"Dear God, you know how weary we feel, how hurt we are, and you cheer us up with your love, your steadfastness, and your precious Word. Thank you, Lord! Amen."

PIT STOP COMING UP!

Sheila Walsh

So then, banish anxiety from your heart
and cast off the troubles of your body.
ECCLESIASTES 11:10

If you're speeding down the freeway, the police might pull you over. But no one ever makes you take pit stops. You have to choose them. It's the same with life. Emergencies force us to stop, but pit stops of joy are events we plan for and savor.

My husband, Barry, and I plan them frequently. We have a list of activities for when the walls close in on us, when we've not had much sleep because our baby Christian is teething, when it's been a tough week, or when it has rained for the last ten days. We turn to a few friends on videotape.

One of our friends is Hyacinth Bucket. Hyacinth is the main character in a British television comedy series on PBS called *Keeping Up Appearances*. She is ridiculously pretentious and surrounded by a cast of hilarious friends and family members. Her brother-in-law sees "no point in getting out of bed if we're all going to die one day anyway." Her long-suffering husband has been "gifted" with early retirement and now has Hyacinth-filled days. The vicar of her church runs every time he sees her coming but never gets away, and the neighbor always spills her coffee on the carpet because Hyacinth makes her nervous.

Every now and then Barry and I will look at each other and say, "This is a Hyacinth moment." He'll grab a bag of chips and salsa. I'll make some hot tea and haul a sack of chocolate chip cookies over to the television set. We'll stick in a tape and laugh till our cheeks ache.

It's good to let go and laugh when life is weighing you down. It won't change any of the circumstances you find yourself in, but when you can laugh at the antics of others, it helps to lighten the load.

Does something come to mind for you? It could be an old black-and-white episode of Andy Griffith or the time Lucy and Ethel worked in the chocolate factory. It might be a video of family and friends that makes you laugh when you watch it. Or maybe it's an old tearjerker movie with a happy ending. Pop in the tape, stock up on the snacks, and put your feet up. There's nothing like a vat of praline pecan ice cream and a good video when the bills are due, the laundry is piled to the ceiling, and the cat just coughed up a fur ball on the dog!

"Lord, today I thank you for pit stops of joy. Thank you for time to stop and laugh, unwind, and cast off my cares. I choose to do this today. In Jesus' name, Amen."

PLAYFUL PEOPLE

Marilyn Meberg

But Jesus called the children to him and said,
"Let the little children come to me, and do not hinder
them, for the kingdom of God belongs to such as these."
LUKE 18:16

I love playful people! People who aren't too sophisticated or too proper to engage in zany antics draw me like a two-year-old to mud. Ken Meberg was such a person.

One of my favorite exchanges of play with him revolved around an Ajax sticker—you know, the one that covers those little holes in the top of the cleanser can.

That sticker caught my attention one night as I was cleaning the sink. Removing the sticker, I thought it really hadn't seen the last of its usefulness. It was so sturdy and full of "stick-um," it seemed a waste to just toss it into the trash.

Carrying it into the bedroom, I took a guess as to which pair of slacks Ken would wear to work the next day and then placed the sticker on the inside pant leg just low enough so he wouldn't be protected by an undergarment but high enough so any overt hand movement in the direction of the sticker would appear indelicate.

According to my expectations, the next day Ken wore the slacks I had "stickered" but said absolutely nothing about it when he came home. I was dying of curiosity, especially since I knew he was chairing a meeting that required him to stand in front of people most of the day. But I contained myself and didn't ask.

After he had changed his clothes and was in the backyard with our son, Jeff, I tore into the bedroom and checked his slacks. The sticker was gone.

Several weeks later I was speaking at a luncheon and became increasingly aware of a scraping irritation in my right armpit. No amount of subtle movement seemed to bring relief, but to scratch or claw at my underarm seemed ill advised since I was surrounded by rather classy ladies who probably had never yielded to a scratch impulse in their lives. Later, at home, I discovered the strategically placed Ajax sticker in the underarm portion of my silk blouse.

This game went on for weeks with neither of us knowing where or when the sticker would appear. My favorite appearance occurred when a policeman stopped Ken for going through a yellow light that turned red while he was in the intersection. When Ken showed his driver's license to the policeman, he laughed and said, "You really must hate your DMV photo."

"Well, not really . . ."

"Then why is your face covered up with some sort of sticker?"

Several days later Ken walked into the kitchen holding the limp sticker by one corner and with mock seriousness announced that the sticker had died; it had no more "stickum." Only then did we settle into a raucous description of our individual experiences with the sticker.

Sometimes I think we responsible adults assume that being playful might be interpreted as being childish, maybe even silly. Admittedly, nothing is more tragic than an adult who fails to gain the maturity and wisdom necessary to live a productive life. But equally tragic are adults who forget how to vent their play instincts.

As in all arenas of successful living, we attempt to work toward a balance. The Danish philosopher Kierkegaard maintains that what we want to remember in living is that "we all possess a child-like quality, but we do not want to be possessed with that quality." To give heedless expression to our childlike impulses is no more desirable than totally to suppress them. The mature person is able to recognize the distinction between the two worlds and choose which world is appropriate for the moment.

Jesus said it's impossible to enter the Kingdom unless we become as little children (Mark 10:15). He seemed to place a high premium on that childlike quality. The most profound truth in the universe is that God loves us; yet many miss that truth because of its simplicity. When Jesus said, "I praise you, Father, Lord of heaven and earth, because you have hidden these things from the wise and learned, and revealed them to little children" (Matthew 11:25), he reminds us of how preferable it is at times to be childlike.

"Lord, we thank you that you have created each of us with a childlike spirit that is capable of fascination, wonder, and enthusiasm. Teach us to revel in that simplicity and in that freedom, to trust you and to take you at your word. Amen."

TILT STEERING

Seeing Life from a Different Angle

THE FABULOUS FEAST

Sheila Walsh

However, as it is written: "No eye has seen, no ear has heard, no mind has conceived what God has prepared for those who love him."

I CORINTHIANS 2:9

As a child, I found it hard to work up any excitement about heaven because I had a sneaking feeling we would all stand around the throne singing "Kum-Ba-Yah" five million times. That's as crazy as . . . well, imagine this.

It was a beautiful night for a banquet. The sky was crystal clear, and the stars sparkled as if freshly polished for the occasion. Delivery vans had been arriving all day. Fresh flowers, crystal glasses, and silver candelabra were carefully placed inside the green and white striped marquee. A team of the best chefs in the area had been hired for the evening, and months of planning had gone into every detail to ensure this would be the social event of the year.

At the last minute, Peter Snow had been hired to act as master of ceremonies. Struggling into his tuxedo, he called to his wife to start the car. He placed a quick kiss on her cheek and was off. It was 7:45 when he pulled into the driveway.

John Ramsey's assistant was waiting for him. "Thank goodness you're here!" she cried. "I was beginning to think you were lost." She turned and disappeared through an impressive set of doors. Peter mumbled something about traffic and lights as he tried to keep up with her.

"Food is in there," she said, pointing through an archway. "Acquaint yourself with the menu. Mr. Ramsey would like you to announce this evening's meal as you call the guests to dinner." Then she was gone.

Peter checked his hair and his bow tie in a gilt mirror, then entered the dining hall. The table was covered with delicate porcelain soup bowls filled with a clear broth, which on investigation proved to be a pheasant consommé. The smell was heavenly. But it was the only dish in sight.

This can't be right! he thought. *Soup?* He'd heard the Ramseys were eccentric, but this was taking it a bit far.

"It's time, it's time!" As quickly as the assistant had disappeared, she was back.

Peter followed her into the garden, beautifully lit with torches and candles. As he was escorted to a raised podium, the assistant signaled for the orchestra to stop playing. Peter marched professionally to the top step, turned around, and cleared his throat. Feeling a bit foolish, he announced in his best toastmaster's voice: "Ladies and gentlemen, if I may have your attention please. Dinner is now being served. The menu this evening, tastefully chosen by the Ramseys, is a delightful pheasant consommé."

There was silence as everyone waited to hear what other gastronomic wonders awaited them. But as Peter descended the steps, the guests began filtering into the dining hall, muttering to each other as they walked.

"What on earth possessed you?" Ramsey hissed under his breath, as he pulled Peter to one side.

"I was shown into the room with the food, sir," he replied. "That's all that there was!"

"That was just the first room!" he cried. "There are five rooms beyond that!"

I write this fanciful story to remind us that we have not even begun to see what God has in store for us. Even the best moments that he showers on us are hardly the appetizer for the banquet he has prepared. In our most exuberant outbursts of love and enthusiasm, we are little more than that master of ceremonies who missed the whole meal. Hold on to your hats, girls, we've only just begun to experience all the delights God has prepared for us!

"Thank you, Father, that you love us and have prepared for us a life with you that our wildest imagination could never do justice to. What joy! Amen."

TREASURED DIFFERENCES

Patsy Clairmont

Male and female he created them.

GENESIS 1:27

"Look, honey! Over here, look!" My husband, Les, excitedly called to me. We had been strolling in our hamlet-sized town, window browsing, when he beckoned me. As I approached to see what he had discovered, I noticed he was pointing down at the sidewalk. That's when I stopped in my tracks. There, at his feet, was a dead, squashed mouse.

"Are you crazy or something?" I shot back at him. "Why would I want to see a dead varmint? Have you ever heard me request to see such a disgusting sight? I'm out of here!"

Les lingered over his find as if he hated to leave it. Yikes! Talk about a tilted steering wheel. Men have such a different angle of viewing things than women. We girls call to others to come see a playful puppy, a cuddly kitten, or a cooing baby.

Meanwhile the guys dangle a grass snake like a charm bracelet, point out the newest road kill, and burp loud enough to register 6.3 on the Richter scale.

That's not to say all guys—just a fair portion—go for the yucky stuff of life. But I find the he-men in my vicinity would rather investigate a spider's nest than check out the new lace curtains.

I'm usually grateful that men's angle of viewing is different. But there are times when I agree with the book title that proclaimed, *Men Are from Mars, Women Are from Venus*. Even though we did start out in the same garden, we don't seem to be smelling the same rosebush.

I find it helpful to gain another's perspective; yet at times when I ask my husband for his, I not only don't get his tilt, but we've ended up in some all-out, big-time bouts.

Speaking of bouts, do any of the men in your life watch *Big Time Wrestling*? Talk about Mars—these are planetary goof balls, sportin' crater-sized 'tudes, pouncing on each other while yelling degrading messages. What a sport! No, make that spout. For these are oversized louts who spout and pout.

Actually, my husband is a sport. He frequently goes along with me while I shop for a new outfit and gives me his perspective, which I value because I want him to enjoy how I look. Of course, we don't always concur on clothes. Sometimes we wrestle over selections. (I wish I knew how to do a half nelson.)

We were drawn to each other in the beginning because we didn't agree on many things. Our differences enable us to enlarge each other's angle of viewing life.

Les was from a large family; I was from a small family. His siblings were clustered in age while my brother, sister, and I were spaced a decade or more apart. Needless to say, we related differently in our families. Therefore, we both brought into our marriage our own expectations of family life. It took time and mistakes to come up with an integrated plan that worked for us. Les and I still have a couple of points of contention in our family theology, but we've learned to work around and even through them.

A common, faulty belief holds that true love and romance means harmony of thought. Whereas I'm of the opinion, if we agree on everything, one of us is unnecessary. We have also given up our contribution to the relationship. Besides, I have seen far too many silent partners wake up one day and walk out. To survive without conflict they had moved so far away from their own leanings, interests, beliefs, opinions, and feelings that, when they got back in touch with themselves, they moved away from their mates. The once cooperative mate now doesn't want the static or hard work required to realign the relationship and therefore finds it easier to begin anew with someone who appreciates his or her slant on life.

We need to respect our differing views (not necessarily because the point has merit but because the person does) and to value another's contribution. I will never—hear me on this—never enjoy viewing mushed mice. But I also don't expect Les to get into girl stuff (tea parties, burping Tupperware, sudden bursts of tears).

"Lord, thank you that you didn't use a cookie cutter when you designed us. Instead, we are handmade, one of a kind, male and female. May we treasure each other's uniqueness and remember to tilt our steering wheels to see from another angle. Amen."

DOT-TO-DOT LIVING

Barbara Johnson

"For I know the plans I have for you," declares the LORD, "plans to prosper you and not to harm you, plans to give you hope and a future."

JEREMIAH 29:11

My darling daughter-in-love, Shannon, says life is like a dot-to-dot picture. When you begin, you have no idea what your life is going to turn out to be. You start at one dot, and then another dot appears, and, hoping for the best, you jump off the first dot to land on the next one.

Sometimes a dot can be a huge, black hole. And other times, the dot is empty, like a zero with the rim rubbed out. Occasionally, dots are tear-shaped. On others you feel like dancing—maybe those are the polka dots!

You have to be well along in life before the big picture becomes apparent. Even then, just when you think you have it figured out, the next dot can pull you way off to the edge—or even over the edge—and then you realize this isn't the picture you thought it was. Not at all.

Sometimes the dots are arranged in a twisted way that makes no sense, and you wonder where on earth this life is taking you. You think maybe you're lost. You imagine that there is no big picture, that you're trudging along on this stupid dot trail and you're never going to get back to the source so the picture can be completed.

Some dots have different shapes; some are stretched into a smile, and others have the form of a heart. How you love those dots! But they're hard to leave, those little lighthearted dots, and you find yourself clinging to them, unwilling to let go, until suddenly they vanish from underneath your feet, and you flail and grope pitifully through the nothingness left beneath you until finally you gain another foothold.

Sometimes you're afraid to step off a dot that's become comfortable and familiar. You look out across the wide expanse of challenges, and you wonder if you'll even make it to the next dot. It takes courage to leap across the vast unknown to land on a strange and foreign dot.

Then there comes a big, black dot that is all-encompassing in its darkness. In fact, it's not a dot at all but a vast sea of black that stretches endlessly in all directions. Sinking into the gloom, you realize there's no way out. You struggle and fight, but there's only more darkness. Finally you give up, unable to struggle through the inky pit of despair one more moment.

It is at that point, says Shannon, that another dot appears. In the vast universe of blackness, it is white—a tiny, glowing pinpoint of light. The light is God, and the beam it casts is his rope of rescue. You wrap its warmth around you, cling to it, and feel yourself rising out of the blackness.

Then, standing beside God in all his glory, at last you can see the picture, a line that continues from dot to dot, forming a life. "Oh, Father!" you cry, turning to thank him for this moment of clarity. It is then that you see what he holds in his hand—an artist's paintbrush. And on its fine-tipped bristles clings a tiny dot of ink.

"Dear Father, you already know every moment of my life, from beginning to end. Thank you for being a lamp for my feet and a light for my path. Amen."

THE EYES OF THE HEART

Luci Swindoll

The LORD does not look at the things man looks at. Man looks at the outward appearance, but the LORD looks at the heart.

1 SAMUEL 16:7

The filthy station wagon pulled into the car wash, loaded with kids and a driver who looked as if he hadn't shaved in weeks. With his hair tousled and a cigarette hanging out of the right side of his mouth, he was wearing clothes he probably had slept in. When he stopped, all eyes turned toward him.

Hairy Dicer, if I ever saw one, I thought to myself. A friend of mine called anybody "Hairy Dicer" who had those little fur dice hanging from his rearview mirror. This guy took the prize.

He opened the back of the wagon and began to lift out the occupants. One by one he hugged and kissed each child, whom he gently lowered to the ground. Then they romped and played with one another and their father to their little hearts' content. I knew they were his children because over and over they called him "Daddy."

"Oh, Daddy, play with us. Daddy, throw me the ball. Look, Daddy, look at this. I can do that, Daddy . . . watch!"

Slowly, lovingly, deliberately, this disheveled man gave attention to all six children, playing, talking, laughing, discovering . . . and together they had a wonderful time. I sat, astonished and ashamed of myself for thinking the guy was a creep.

How quickly we judge another's outward appearance. It's so easy to do, isn't it? We see clothes that don't match, and we judge. We don't like a person's hair so we judge. We look at another's car, manners, music, posture, or facial characteristics . . . judging all the while.

I'll tell you, if the human perspective had been the criterion for God's judgment, the Swindolls would have been zapped long ago. Each of us, my brothers and I, live the majority of our lives in well-worn clothes that don't match. Comfortable is what we like. More often than not, I go to the store in my oldest sweats. They're perfect. They fit the contours of my aging body and feel great. I don't want to change clothes just to pick up a carton of milk, grab a hamburger, or have the car washed. My friends encourage me to wear designer sweats. Not on your life!

In Antoine de Saint-Exupéry's book, *The Little Prince*, he states the principle, "It is only with the heart that one can see rightly; what is essential is invisible to the eye."

Oh, how I love that thought. "What is essential is invisible" captures what we read in Scripture. Not only do we have no right to pass judgment on another, but we also have no way to see what's inside that person.

Who cares if the guy at the car wash was the opposite of my view of a proper dad? All those kids cared about was the attention he gave them. He listened. He played. He loved them.

And, you know what is really amazing? When I saw his heart . . . with my heart . . . he became almost good-looking. Well, maybe not good-looking, but certainly more appealing. I saw him with different eyes, the eyes of nonjudgment. I liked him.

When I don't put any judgmental demands on others, I'm happiest because I know I'm doing what is right. I feel good. When nobody puts demands on me, it frees me to be who I really am—a slob, clothed in Christ's righteousness.

"Oh, Father, help us be obedient to your Word, which says to accept one another as you, in Christ Jesus, have accepted us. Amen."

THE ROAD TO GLORY AIN'T ALWAYS EASY

Thelma Wells

In this world you will have trouble. But take heart!
I have overcome the world.

JOHN 16:33

One of the most glorious experiences I've ever had is to travel in the Holy Land. A pastor asked me to be the soloist on a trip he was organizing, and after I gladly accepted, twenty-three of my family members and friends joined the entourage.

Everywhere we went brought Bible stories to life, but a couple of Holy Land experiences especially stood out for me. The first was watching my daughter Vikki climb the mountain at Masada. It was a frightening moment for her and me. Vikki, with her free spirit, discovered that once you start to climb a mountain, it's so steep and rough your only option is to keep your sights on finishing and your mind on the rocks and boulders up ahead. You have to keep looking forward and not back, and you have to pray every step of the way that you will make it.

It took Vikki so long to reach the top where the group was waiting for her that I was worried. Others who had started up the mountain with her had arrived looking wild-eyed and fatigued, saying that was not a wise choice. They wished they had ridden the cable cars as most of us had.

When I asked if they had seen Vikki, they said she was having difficulty climbing the mountain, but all of them were in distress and nobody could help anyone else. You can imagine how that made me feel.

Vikki finally arrived at the top. Many of our group were cheering and thanking God that she had survived the ordeal. Vikki's first words were, "Mama, don't ever let me do something like that again. I thought I was going to die!"

That experience taught her the road to glory is difficult with its rocks and boulders, its strain and struggle. But if you keep on keeping on, you can make it. Things aren't always as easy as we would like. Surprises and pitfalls wait for us along the road of life. We're going to sweat and sway, we're going to wonder why things are the way they are, and we're even going to blame other people.

But every road has an end; every mountain has its peak. If we can just hold on and keep climbing, knowing that God is aware of how we're straining, he will bring us over and up the mountains. It's consoling to know God is in control of every part of our journey to glory, even over the steep mountains.

The second experience that especially touched my soul was walking down the Via Dolorosa (The Way of Sorrows) where Jesus painfully walked, carrying his cross and passing by Simon the Cyrene, the man who helped Jesus bear the cross up Golgotha.

But this moving experience turned into a nightmare for one of the pastors traveling with us. He had been to the Holy Land more than twenty-five times and had warned us about pickpockets in the Via Dolorosa crowd and how skillfully they committed their crime. He told us to keep our money on our bodies rather than in purses or satchels. The men should keep their wallets out of their back pockets. He cautioned us to take off any precious jewelry and dress down to keep from being pegged as "rich" tourists. All of us obeyed.

Once a person's belongings were gone, the pastor warned, it would be extremely difficult to catch who did it because the thieves would mingle in the crowd.

The man who had given us these explicit instructions was our only casualty. He had his hand in his pocket holding his money clip inside his passport when a skillful pickpocket whisked his hand into that pocket, taking the passport and the money. The preacher saw nothing. He felt the heist, but it was too late.

The victim preacher told us he had become too sure of himself. He thought he had traveled enough and knew how to keep himself safe.

Doesn't the same thing happen in life? God warns us of danger. We listen and are careful. But then we slough off. Even when we see warning signs, we think we're smart enough and have our act together. We don't listen or pay attention. That's when we fall and fail.

So whether you're climbing mountains or think you have a firm grip on everything that's important to you, you would be wise to look to the Lord. Remain humble and aware that your footing could slip at any time—or you could feel those things that are so precious to you slip out from your fingers without warning. We're on the way to glory land, but we ain't there yet!

"Lord, thank you that you give us the endurance to climb every mountain in our path to glory. Help us to keep our eyes fixed on you through it all. And thank you that even when the going gets tough you give us sweet contentment in our souls. Enable us to keep our ears attuned to your warnings for us and not to become cocky or complacent when we think we know the way ahead. Thank you for the protection you extend to us when we listen. Amen."

PARTY OF FOUR
Marilyn Meberg

Therefore be clear minded and self-controlled.

1 PETER 4:7

Last night I had the fun of buying my grandson Ian his first tricycle. Feeling celebratory, I asked my friend Pat, who had accompanied me on this excursion, if she felt like popping into the pizza place across the parking lot and taking a pizza to my house.

Neither of us was prepared for the inefficiency and confusion that characterized every young person working at the restaurant. After we had waited fifteen minutes to place our order, four different people eventually made an effort to attend to it. With difficulty, one person finally understood that I didn't want two but only one medium pepperoni pizza with thin crust. Another worker asked if it was "for here or to go" while someone else gave me change from my twenty-dollar bill. Yet another worker with sauce on his wrist asked if I'd like to see a menu.

Leaning on the "Please Wait to Be Seated Sign," I asked Pat if she saw anything on the walls stating "We hire the incompetent." Seeing nothing, we decided they hadn't gotten around to posting their policy yet.

Oddly enough, either through ignorance or compassion about the restaurant policy, people started to pour in the front door and stood about waiting to be seated. Since none of the confused workers felt inclined to host, I thought it only charitable to help out. Grabbing a few menus, I asked the two people at the head of the line to please follow me, and I'd be happy to seat them. Then, after seating a party of four, I noticed Pat had disappeared. I spotted her seating a party of three on the other side of the salad bar. Relieved to have cleared out our waiting space, we settled in to wait for our pizza.

Ten minutes later Pat nudged me. "Marilyn, that party of four you seated over by the window is pointing at you and looking pretty hostile."

"They probably don't know the restaurant policy. Maybe I should go tell them." I walked over to their table hoping to diffuse their anger.

One of the men, in an argumentative tone, asked, "Do you work here?"

"Well, actually, no. I was waiting for my pizza."

"Why did you seat us?"

"Somebody needed to."

The couple sitting at the table next to this crabby foursome, and whom I had seated first, were smiling broadly as they listened to this exchange. "We wondered why a hostess was wearing jeans and a sweatshirt," the woman said, "but we were more interested in sitting down than inquiring about your uniform."

At that moment my name was called, and amazingly enough, I was handed one medium, pepperoni pizza with thin crust. I walked over to the fun couple and said, "I just paid ten dollars for this pepperoni pizza. I'll sell it to you for twelve."

"Does it have anchovies?"

"If it had anchovies, I'd give it to you!" We laughed and they thanked me for at least a place to sit and said they would leave in a few more minutes to go down the street to Coco's.

Glancing at the still glowering party of four, I said, "Your waitress should be with you any day now. Enjoy your meal." I then bolted for the door.

Pat and I giggled all the way home over that crazy interlude. We agreed that the foursome had appeared crabby when they walked in. It wasn't just the lack of service or even my obnoxious behavior that set them off. They undoubtedly lived their lives in a state of perpetual annoyance.

Choosing not to be annoyed by life's annoyances is admittedly difficult at times. I often have to remind myself that I have a choice in how I'm going to respond. I'm not talking about denying my feelings and stuffing them away so they can later come back as a headache or a mystifying body rash. I'm suggesting that once I identify the feeling, I can choose to take control of it instead of its taking control of me. I'm also talking about those pesky annoyances that have the potential to join forces so that by the end of the day they have become one big party of four.

First Peter 4:7 reminds me to be clear minded and self-controlled. If my mind becomes cluttered by the day's annoyances, it's a given that sooner or later I'm going to lose my self-control. If I lose my self-control, for sure I'm going to lose my joy. I hate losing my joy. Fortunately, I have a choice in how I react; just like I have a choice in where *not* to go for pizza.

"Thanks for reminding me, Lord, that I don't have to let the small stuff rob me of joy. When I keep my mind centered on who you are and who you are to me, it settles me down and enables me to smile instead of frown. Keep me ever mindful of your loving support through the annoying events of each day. May I reflect who you are instead of who I am. Amen."

FRIENDLY SKIES

Patsy Clairmont

As the heavens are higher than the earth, so are my ways higher than your ways.

ISAIAH 55:9

I had a 'tude the size of a B52 (a World War II bomber). You see, I wasn't all that thrilled about flying. If the good Lord had meant for us to be up in the air, he would have required us to live in hangars instead of homes.

What prompted my 'tude wasn't just the altitude, the confinement, or the six peanuts they serve as a meal (I give more generous snacks to our family dog). No, it was much more than that.

I can't even say it was the people who board and casually whack off the top of your head with their slung-over-the-shoulder carry-ons as they obliviously bebop down the aisle to locate their seats. (Doesn't bother me, doesn't bother me, doesn't bother me.) Nor do I believe my 'tude inflated simply because of the telephone-booth-size rest rooms that allow you to back in and sidle out. It wasn't even the towel disposal bin, whose location remains a mystery to me.

No, I think my greater gripe was when the 'tude barons boarded. These are the folks who enter the plane with the idea this confined space is theirs to do with as they please. The ones who shove their belongings under your seat, who elbow you repeatedly to expand their comfort, and who talk so loud they can be heard throughout the plane, if not the firmament. Some believe a restricted space with recirculated air is the best place to apply their nail polish or spray a fresh mist of perfume upon their person (never mind the hyperventilating asthmatic next to them).

Yes, all these things gave me a high-flyin' 'tude. Then one day I realized navigating the airways was to be a constant part of my life, and I was going to lose my joy a lot if I didn't make some altitude adjustments. I needed another perspective.

When I'm willing to view my situations from another angle, often details come into focus I hadn't really thought about before. In fact, once I refocused on my frequent flying, I came up with this list of reasons I'm grateful to be airborne. I'll put on a grati-'tude before boarding because:

1. It provides a way to travel that allows me to dart about the country and do things I could never do otherwise.
2. I've met wonderful people not only after I arrive at my destination but also in the skies (well, most of those people).
3. I can sit down, be still, and maybe even slip in a nap.
4. I have a chance to catch up on some good reading.
5. I have opportunities to be light and salt to an often dark and unseasoned world.
6. I might be able to offer a word of kindness to an anxious traveler or a stressed flight attendant.
7. As unskilled at cooking as I am, I can still offer up a better meal than the airlines.

These are just some of the reasons that caused me to tilt my steering wheel to a different angle so I could see around my attitudes. Now, how about you? Need a new flight plan? Maybe you don't have to take on the friendly skies but instead find yourself taxiing around your home or office with a jet-sized 'tude. Try sitting still (which is hard to do with a revving 'tude) and ask the Lord for a fresh perspective for an old flight pattern or routine. Then prepare for takeoff (bring seat to an upright position, fasten seat belt, stow tray table) and enjoy the amazing view.

"Lord, steer me clear of myself long enough that I might gain sight of a higher plan. Amen."

FIRE!

Thelma Wells

But select capable men from all the people—
men who fear God, trustworthy men who hate
dishonest gain—and appoint them as officials
over thousands, hundreds, fifties and tens.

Exodus 18:21

I've heard people say, "If you want anything done right, you have to do it yourself."

I used to say that, too, until I realized I didn't have a life because I had so many fires to put out, and someone always seemed to be pouring on more fuel. The stress was overwhelming. My smoke screen of rationalizations for why I needed to be the one to do all those tasks was fast disappearing. I needed help.

As in putting out any fire that's out of hand, I couldn't do this alone. I enlisted the help of others by pledging to myself I would teach appropriate people everything I knew about what I was doing. Projects that used to be mine became ours. Clients I thought only I could handle were delegated to staff. Records I had to have my hands on at all times became the responsibility of others.

Now everyone knows how the system works and is able to keep it going despite a hectic work schedule, deadlines, and putting out those fires.... Come to think of it, we don't have many fires to put out because the system works so well. What a relief to know I can travel, take vacations, write books—things that take me away from the office weeks at a time—and still have a well-run business.

I'm not the first to experience the suffocating effects of thinking I have to do it all to get it right. Nor am I the first to think about delegating as a way to pour water on the fire. Moses' father-in-law, Jethro, saw that he was stressed to the max because he was judging, managing, controlling, budgeting, pastoring, teaching, preaching, and being everything to everybody on the journey from Egypt to the Promised Land. So he told Moses that he needed to delegate a big chunk of his responsibilities. He was a behind-the-scenes fire chief, quietly seeing to it that all the appropriate fire trucks and firefighters were dispatched to bring Moses some relief.

Maybe you have said you need help with all the fires raging in your life: projects at home, work, and church; responsibilities with your friends, family, and coworkers; a calendar filled to bursting. You might have said you would rather do it yourself to make sure it's done right. But one of the most rewarding ways to relate to others is to give them ownership over what's going on. At home the entire family should share in keeping things up around the house. At work people want to be a part of things and to have responsibility with accountability. And others in your life are waiting for you to take some items off your calendar so you have time to spend with them.

First, you have to decide you're tired of fighting these blazes yourself. Then you need to decide who can help and how. Form a bucket brigade and get everyone to pitch in.

Now, one caveat is important to recognize. You have to remember that delegation has few short-term benefits but amazing long-term benefits. You see, it takes awhile to complete the delegation process. Training, explaining, and overseeing are all part of it. However, when everyone has tasks and can do them with little supervision, you begin to reap the results and feel relief.

I bet that you have some people to whom you can delegate housework, office work, and church work. Wouldn't it be great not to have the frightening words, "Fire! Another fire!" reverberating in your mind?

"Oh, Lord, when you gave Moses the pattern for delegation and proved over the centuries it can work, it stands to reason that I should follow that pattern when appropriate. Praise you, Lord, that you provide ways for us to be more productive and less stressed. Help me to trust people enough to give them important tasks. Help those to whom I delegate accept the responsibility with confidence and commitment to do a superior job. Amen."

RUDE AWAKENING

Sheila Walsh

Weeping may remain for a night,
but rejoicing comes in the morning.
PSALM 30:5

I have never been a morning person, so it was a rude awakening when baby Christian came along. I remember saying to my mom that I would need to buy a new alarm clock so I could wake up and feed the baby. She laughed. I didn't know then that babies come fully equipped with their own, not-to-be-ignored alarm.

As Christians, we all are morning people. We live now, as C. S. Lewis said, in the shadowlands, and we wait for morning.

I can think of many "shadowy" moments in my life. And I know, if we could see the joy of the morning, we would make it through those dark nights. I think about how differently I would have handled my dark time if Christ had handed me my baby boy and said, "Sheila, this is your son. He won't be born for a few more years. Now look at him. He needs you to find courage to get up and get emotionally well." How much easier it would have been to hold that precious life, look into those eyes, and find a reason to go on. But that didn't happen. Instead, Christ was there. And he asked me to get well and to believe, in faith, that he would make the crooked in my life straight.

So it was that Christian came into my life, bringing the joy of the morning to Barry and me. My delivery was easy compared to some horror stories I had heard, but it was quite enough for me. Barry and I had faithfully attended childbirth classes, and I had practiced breathing until I was hyperventilating. The nurse who had taught the class walked us through the various transition stages of labor and the breathing that would be appropriate for each stage. I have since decided she was actually a nightclub comedian in disguise because what she told us was a joke.

Christian wasn't due until the end of December, but at my checkup on December 12, pains hit me out of nowhere. Fortunately, my doctor's office was right next door to the hospital, and I was admitted immediately.

"What happened to the transitions?" I wailed to my husband. "I'll sue that nurse."

"Keep breathing, honey," Barry said lovingly. "You're doing great."

"Doing great! Are you kidding?" I replied. "Come over here and say that, and you'll be lucky if you ever breathe again!"

But Barry was too busy putting on a Christmas CD he thought would help me relax. I still have vivid memories of lying on a bed in the most excruciating pain I have ever experienced and hearing, "Just hear those sleigh bells jing-a-ling, ting-ting-ting-a-ling too."

At 5:20 A.M., December 13, Christian Walsh Pfaehler came bursting into the world at seven pounds, eight ounces. It's impossible to put into words the emotions that washed over me in great waves as I looked into the eyes of this little lamb we had prayed for for so long.

At 9:00 that evening the nurse sent Barry home and told me to get some sleep. She gave me a strong painkiller the doctor had prescribed, and I fell asleep almost immediately.

I woke up with a start. I looked at the clock and saw it was midnight. Where was I, and what was that funny noise beside me? I sat up too quickly, and my head spun. I looked to my left and located the funny noise. Apparently it was hungry. I wasn't sure what to do. I eased myself out of the bed, bent over the crib, and picked up my boy.

"I want to apologize if I don't get this right at first," I said as he stared up at me. "I'm a beginner, and I'm really not sure what I'm doing."

I took him into bed with me, and he nestled in.

"I'm kind of old to be a first-time mom, but I promise you I'll do my best."

He seemed oblivious to our first talk, but I carried on anyway. "But the best thing that we have going for us, Little Lamb, is that Jesus loves us both, and he'll help us." I looked down, but he was asleep, and in a few moments so was I.

Whatever you're going through at the moment, remember this is not the end of your story. We are morning people, called to live by faith and not by sight, to lift our hearts to God in the darkness because we have the promise of the morning.

"Lord,
In the darkness be my light
In the silence be my song
In the stillness be my hope.
Amen."

FIVE-FINGER EXERCISE

Luci Swindoll

Whoever can be trusted with very little can also be trusted with much, and whoever is dishonest with very little will also be dishonest with much. So if you have not been trustworthy in handling worldly wealth, who will trust you with true riches?

LUKE 16:10–11

I'd studied the models in the hobby shop window for days. Three balsa airplanes. Seven bucks. Where was I going to get the money? My allowance wasn't quite enough. Finally, borrowing from one of my brothers, I ran to the store, bought the models, and hurried home to show my parents. I spread everything out on the table and explained how I was going to carve, build, and paint these cute little airplanes. I couldn't wait to start.

"Just a minute," Mother said. "How much did they cost?"

"Seven dollars and fifty cents. I saved the seven and borrowed fifty cents from Babe."

Then my father joined the discussion. "Did you spend all the money you had on models?"

"Yes, sir."

Calmly, but with a serious expression, Daddy said, "Honey, buying models isn't a bad thing. They're fun to make, and I'm sure you'll enjoy them. But spending everything you have on one purchase is not wise. Someday, when you're grown, you are going to be responsible for your own money. If you use it carefully, you'll always have some."

Then he opened his hand, and pointing to each finger as he stated each principle, he said, "Spend some, save some, tithe some, invest some, and give some away. If you do this, you'll never have to worry about money."

That was my first course in stewardship. I was ten. And now, I remember his lesson. When applied, I can tell you it works.

Money is a medium of exchange. It's the tool with which we barter. It enables us to do things. To own things. To enjoy things. It is not an end in itself; it's a means to an end. When we keep that straight, we'll resolve much of the angst we experience regarding money.

God instructs us to be good stewards, and when we obey this instruction, money is not a problem. Read Luke 16:10–11 again. It says if you're a good steward of little, you can be trusted with more. Even much.

I follow simple but practical principles about handling money. These guidelines help me make wise financial choices. They help me control my money without it controlling me.

1. Tithe off my gross income.
2. Live within my means.
3. Take care of what I have.
4. Wear it out.
5. Do it myself.
6. Anticipate my needs.
7. Consider multiple use.
8. Make gifts.
9. Shop less.
10. Buy used.
11. Pay cash.
12. Do without.

Let me give you three other suggestions that I find helpful: First, if the pleasure of having something is sweeter to you than the pain of paying it off, don't be afraid of indebtedness. But you must manage it.

Second, if you see others affording things you can't, stop comparing. Scripture says when we compare ourselves, we are not wise.

Third, if you want to be the happiest person in town, give away more than you keep. It is indeed more blessed (joyful) to give than to receive.

As a daughter of the King, remember this: No matter how little money is in your purse, you're already rich anyway. You may be broke, but you'll never be poor.

"Loving Father, give me what it takes to take care of what you give me. And help me to remember everything I have is yours. Amen."

BOUNTIFUL BLESSINGS

Barbara Johnson

Do not repay evil with evil or insult with insult, but with blessing, because to this you were called so that you may inherit a blessing.

I PETER 3:9

A man named Sebastian decided to masquerade as a priest to please his dying Aunt Esther, whose fortune he wanted to inherit. She had always hoped he would become a clergyman.

It was all just an act. Sebastian was far from being a godly man. In fact, he was one of those characters people describe as worthless unless sold by the pound. But a strange thing happened whenever he wore his clerical costume. He found himself becoming nicer to others. He left bigger tips in restaurants, even when the food was bad. He was more patient while driving in rush-hour traffic. And people were unexpectedly nice to him in return.

Sebastian, not a Christian at that point, had probably never read God's promise in Proverbs 11:25, "He who refreshes others will himself be refreshed." So Sebastian was surprised by what happened to him. He was so moved by his experiences that eventually he became a real priest. He had discovered the truth in the saying, "Love, like paint, can make things beautiful when you spread it, but it simply dries up when you don't use it."

Sebastian no longer wore a costume; he was clad in the "garment of praise instead of a spirit of despair" (Isaiah 61:3).

Actually, Sebastian is a character in Alfred Alcorn's novel, *Vestments*. Unlike Sebastian, I've found that as God showers me with blessings and as I share them with others, I've received so much love in return that I'm no longer surprised. The rebounding "surprises" have become delightfully dependable.

For example, the people whose lives are touched by Spatula Ministries, the organization Bill and I operate to help parents who are dealing with the death or alienation of their children, often respond by asking how they can help someone else—a perfect example of rebounding blessings. That happened recently when a distraught mother called me from a trailer park in the Northwest. She was going through a very painful time, and she had heard I was coming to a nearby city for a women's seminar.

"Barb, I don't have the money to buy a ticket, but it would help me so much if I could just talk with you a minute," she said. "I know it's a lot to ask, but could you meet me outside the auditorium when you have a spare minute? I'd wait all day if I thought I'd get to see you! And I'd bring my copies of your books for you to sign."

Promising to call her back when the weekend's schedule was finalized, I hung up the phone, my heart aching for the anguished mother. Then, just a few days later, a letter came from another mom in the Northwest who had finally emerged from the tunnel of an especially painful ordeal that had nearly destroyed her life.

She was grateful for all that her new Spatula friends had done for her, and she said she wanted to pass along the blessing that had been shared with her. "What can I do, Barb?" she asked. "How can I help?"

Looking at her letter, something tugged at me, something about her return address. The woman lived in a trailer park, and its name rang a bell in my memory. In a flash I was on the phone to her. "There's a woman who lives in your trailer park, and she could use some encouragement right now."

"I'm on my way," the other mother said excitedly.

Not only did she reach out to the woman who had called me, but she also gave that woman enough money to buy tickets to the seminar, not just for herself but for several friends. As a result, all of us received a special splash of joy that day as we realized how God had reached out to two far-apart corners of our country and brought us all together to refresh each other and share each other's burdens—and blessings.

Ardath Rodale, CEO of Rodale Press, said, "Inhale all the good that surrounds you, and as you exhale, give it away by sharing with others." As you breathe this way, no doubt you'll discover another sage's wise observation: "One of the most beautiful compensations of life is that no one can sincerely try to help another without helping herself."

"Dear God, thank you for all the joyful blessings you have splashed upon my life. Please help me be creative in finding ways I can share those blessings with others. Amen."

ON THE RUN

Marilyn Meberg

I will lie down and sleep in peace, for you alone,
O LORD, make me dwell in safety.

PSALM 4:8

Wherever I go, I generally have a newsmagazine or a book stuffed in my purse in case I have to wait. Since my personality type rarely waits well, I feel pacified knowing I have something to read if I need it.

Some time ago I was waiting in a dental office I had never been to before. Because I had left home hurriedly, I had neglected to grab any reading material. So I found myself voraciously reading everything on the office walls. I was unsettled by a poster near the door entitled, "Every Morning in Africa." It said,

Every morning in Africa a gazelle wakes up,
It knows that it must run faster
Than the fastest lion or it will be killed.
Every morning a lion wakes up, it knows
That it must outrun the slowest gazelle or
It will starve to death.
It doesn't matter whether you are a lion or a gazelle:
When the sun comes up
You had better be running.

Noting my discomfort with this message, I began one of my interior monologues to figure out what was going on in me. "What troubles you about those words, Marilyn?"

"I hate that it's true about the gazelle and the lion. That truth feels so hostile. Why does anyone or anything have to live life under such threat. . . . There's no peace."

"That all happened as a result of the Fall in the Garden of Eden. That survivor thing came with the entrance of sin into an otherwise perfect and nonthreatening world. It was then that lions started chasing gazelles."

"I hate the Fall."

"You've mentioned that before, Marilyn. Why do you have to spiritualize everything? You can be a bit of a bore, you know!"

My internal arguing came to an abrupt halt when I was invited to enter the "dental chambers." There I learned the gold crown on the bottom left side of my jaw was slightly cracked, which explained why I was experiencing discomfort; it would cost only 1.5 million dollars to have it repaired. I was tempted to bolt out of the office and run like a gazelle, but I was strapped to the chair via my mouth.

Later, when I made my escape, I pondered again that troublesome poster. Not only did I hate the gazelle-lion dynamic, I hated the imperative that I, too, lived under siege and "when the sun comes up you had better be running." Yet the disturbing reality is, at times, we all appear to be running . . . running literally for our lives. We're running from responsibilities, we're running from hurtful memories, we're running from relationships that require time and discipline to repair, we're running from various fears we think may overtake us, and we're even running from knowledge of ourselves.

Why do we do that? Unfortunately, like the lion and the gazelle, we run because we feel threatened. We run to survive.

In time, the words on that maddening poster led me to some reassuring truths. I don't have to run to survive. As a matter of fact, I am invited to rest to survive. Matthew 11:28 says, "Come to me, all you who are weary and burdened, and I will give you rest."

I can just see myself running into the outstretched arms of the Savior, who recognizes I am weary from running and offers me a place of refuge from all that threatens to overtake me. He offers me rest, and he assures me of that safe, surviving place with him.

Remember that fantastic verse, Deuteronomy 33:27? "The eternal God is your refuge, and underneath are the everlasting arms. He will drive out your enemy before you, saying, 'Destroy him!'" Now that's a powerhouse verse for any of us feeling besieged by lions. We will find refuge in his arms. We will find rest as he enfolds us to himself. He will even destroy our enemies. What tremendous joy those truths inspire for those of us prone to running.

Having finally made peace with that poster, I found myself again sitting in the dental chair. I said, "You know that poster you have on the wall about the lion and the gazelle? Well, I have some thoughts about . . ." In mid-sentence I found myself strapped down, and my mouth filled with nearly everything but the dentist's left shoe.

"Isn't that a great poster," he beamed, continuing to load up my mouth. "I guess you could say that's my basic philosophy for living."

It was then I noticed how hairy his hands, arms, face, and neck were.

"Lord, thank you that you are my safe place, my refuge. Thank you for your invitation to retreat there anytime, anywhere. Amen."

LISTEN TO YOUR HEART

Thelma Wells

My sheep listen to my voice;
I know them, and they follow me.

John 10:27

Do you ever wish you had followed your heart instead of your mind? I do! I wish I had stayed in San Antonio the day after we had finished a Women of Faith conference. We speakers were meeting to discuss plans for 1998, but I had a previous commitment in Lincoln, Nebraska, so I couldn't stay.

Fortunately, I was able to attend the first hour. When Pat, my assistant, came to let me know our ride to the airport was waiting, I thought, *I ought to stay here. I'm not going to Lincoln. I should wait a few minutes.* But then I thought, *Are you crazy? You promised your client in Lincoln you would be there. Suppose you miss the flight? You have to speak at the opening session Monday morning. Git outta here!*

I followed Pat to the waiting car and mentioned to her I thought I should stay. I telephoned my office for messages from the car on the way to the airport. There were none. When I reached the San Antonio airport, I called again. Nothing. In my heart, I still believed I wasn't going to Lincoln.

When I got to my house in Dallas, I turned on the weather channel. What was the first thing I heard? "All power lines are down in Lincoln, Nebraska. This is the worse snowstorm they have had in many years. Travelers' advisories are out all over the state. Airports are closed . . ."

I called my client's home in Lincoln. No answer. I called the hotel where the meeting was scheduled and was informed the meeting had been canceled. I called my office and heard a message that sounded frantic. "Thelma, Thelma, if you have not boarded the plane coming to Lincoln, please, please don't. The program has been canceled. We'll call you when the weather is better to let you know if we rescheduled. I sure hope you get this message." There was a second message, "Thelma, do not come to Lincoln today. Will call you later." Still another message, "Thelma, I am to pick you up at the airport. We have not been able to speak with you personally. I will be there, but I hope you won't."

I unpacked my bags, settled down, and told my husband how I wished I had listened to my heart. If I had stayed at the Women of Faith meeting a little longer and called my office a little later, I could have stayed for the entire meeting. In my heart, I sensed what God wanted me to do, but I was too fearful to respond.

You might ask, "Thelma, how do you know it was God directing you? It could have been you talking to yourself because you wanted to be in the meeting!"

Good question! My experience with the prompting of the Holy Spirit has been that when he does, there is an indescribable peace in your body, mind, and spirit that you feel but can't explain to anyone who hasn't experienced it. And, of course, God's Spirit would never direct us to do anything contrary to Scripture, so we have a guidebook that can help us. You've probably said in certain situations, "I knew in my heart that such and such was . . ." Or, "I had a feeling that . . ." Those are probably times God's Spirit is prompting you.

Even though I didn't go to Lincoln that day, I realized more fully that I need to be responsive to the Holy Spirit. I have found him to be the greatest organizer, time manager, administrator, arbitrator, and scheduler.

What will you do when you think you're being prompted by the Holy Spirit to take a certain action? I'd suggest you ask for clarity. Wait for the answer. I can't tell you how you will know when the answer comes, but I can tell you that you will experience peace in your mind, body, and soul that you can't describe. Listen to your heart.

"Divine Master, help us understand when we hear your voice deep within us. When you speak, remind us that, as your children, we know your voice. Help us to trust your instructions and not to be afraid. Amen."

UP, UP, AND AWAY

Luci Swindoll

For nothing is impossible with God.

LUKE 1:37

It was one of the most exciting things I've ever done. You should see my pictures. There we were, one hundred invited guests gathered in a private area to watch the liftoff of Atlantis. At 10:37 P.M., in clear, balmy Florida, the shuttle soared heavenward. Fire, steam, smoke, clicking cameras, yelling, whistling, shouting . . . and then KA-BOOM! Off they went. I loved that moment. It took my breath away, and I was so proud to be an American.

I was a guest of astronaut Wendy Lawrence, who left Earth for a ten-day mission. Wendy is a woman of strong personal faith in Christ, and I delighted in praying for her and the others before they left. During those days the Atlantis spent in orbit, I was immensely more interested in the space program than ever before. I even went outside every night and looked up just in case I could wave to Wendy. And I prayed for them until they were safely home.

The instant that shuttle lifted off and was so quickly beyond Earth's bonds, I was mesmerized. Talk about defying odds, breaking barriers, not being held back . . . what a graphic illustration! Even the force of gravity did not hold back that little ship.

I know people like that. And, if you'll pardon the pun, I gravitate toward them. They're a source of encouragement to me. They hang tough when others give up, forge ahead when others lag behind, choose to be cheerful when others sink in defeat. People like my friend Charlotte.

Char defies the odds. After multiple surgeries and chronic health problems, she maintains the most incredible attitude. Every time I chat with her on the phone, she is reticent to talk about herself because she's so busy asking about me: "Now where are you? Oh, I've been there, and I love it, too. You say it's snowing? Golly, I remember when I was there, and . . ." Off and running. No self-pity, no martyrdom, no self-centeredness. Her spirit soars, though her body fails. When I hang up, I feel better.

One of the pioneers of Starbucks Coffee Company writes in his book, *Pour Your Heart Into It*, "Once you overcome seemingly insurmountable obstacles, other hurdles become less daunting. Most people can achieve beyond their dreams if they insist upon it. I'd encourage everyone to dream big, lay your foundations well, absorb information like a sponge, and not be afraid to defy conventional wisdom. Just because it hasn't been done before doesn't mean you shouldn't try it."*

I feel the strength of those words as they lift off the page. Yet even more powerful are the words of Jesus, who challenged his followers to move mountains, walk on water, and prepare a picnic for five thousand. He assured us we would do no less than the impossible.

I don't know the circumstances of your life. Maybe, like my friend Charlotte, you have health problems. Maybe you're experiencing a financial crisis, a relational struggle, or a genuine feeling of inadequacy. Whatever your biggest problems, be sure you aren't surrendering to the odds. You may look at yourself and say, "I can't. I can't rise above this, get beyond it, or overcome," and so you give up. Let me say with all the love in the world, my friend, don't quit. You're just starting this ride. You have the whole sky above your head. God wants to free you from bondage, and he knows just how to do it.

---

*Howard Schultz, *Pour Your Heart Into It* (New York: Hyperion, 1997), 19.

"Father, you don't always do exactly what I think you will, but you can do the impossible. Lift my spirits and help me soar. Amen."

SHAGGY FRIENDS

Sheila Walsh

But when you give a banquet, invite the poor,
the crippled, the lame, the blind, and you will be blessed.
Although they cannot repay you, you will be repaid
at the resurrection of the righteous.

LUKE 14:13–14

We rang the doorbell, and the resulting sound of barking and scampering paws on hardwood floors was deafening. I laughed as I looked through the door's glass pane and saw four shaggy dogs running over each other in a desire to be first to the door.

The door opened, and Barry and I got down and greeted our shaggy friends before we even said hello to our hosts, Karalyn and Joe.

"What a menagerie!" Barry said as the smallest dog licked him over and over. We sat in our friends' study drinking iced tea, and eventually the dogs all found their places, flopping down exhausted from extending such an effusive welcome.

"Tell me about the dogs, Karalyn," I said. "You have quite a collection!"

"Well, Anabel came from an abusive home," Karalyn began. "I heard through a friend that this little dog was being beaten and left outside in the cold with nothing to eat, and I decided to do something about it. When we got her home, one of her legs had been broken in five places."

I looked at Anabel peacefully asleep on Joe's lap and found it hard to imagine that people could be so cruel.

"The little white one is having a hard time," Karalyn continued. "He's completely deaf and has a bad back and a sore paw."

Sunday, a hyperventilating Yorkie with a lilac bow in her hair, was getting on in years, and Jackson looked like he was growling till you saw his tail wagging fit to be propelled off his body. I have never seen dogs more loved or cared for than these four.

"Do you make a habit of rescuing dogs from the pound?" I asked.

"Yes, I do," Karalyn answered, smiling at her husband as he shook his head in wonder at his large-hearted wife. "Everyone wants a perfect animal, a new one that looks great with no faults or limitations, but I've found the animals who have been all but tossed away have so much love to give."

Later I thought about what Karalyn had said and related it to people. So often we want to be with the "right" people, the crowd who look and sound like us. Yet Christ said, "Invite the poor, the crippled, the lame, and the blind, and you will be blessed."

I saw that in Karalyn. She is blessed by the love she receives from her tail-wagging friends and by knowing that she has made a difference in lives that needed a miracle.

Christ's story goes on to say that we shouldn't entertain those who can repay us but rather those who have nothing to give. In every church across America there are those who come lonely and leave lonely every Sunday. In each neighborhood, estranged ones live. Old people's homes are full of forgotten lives. No one comes to see these people anymore. I imagine these aged ones watch groups of friends and families talking and laughing together as they head out to eat or to a ball game. What a blessing it would be to them and to us if we really saw them and included them in our lives.

"Lord, you saw me in my nakedness and loved me just the same. You reached me in my sinfulness; I heard you call me friend. So give me eyes to see, I pray, the ones who have no name. Pour your oil on wounded hearts, Christ, on this earth again. Amen."

THE MOST POWERFUL PERFUME

Barbara Johnson

But thanks be to God, who ... through us spreads everywhere the fragrance of the knowledge of him.

2 CORINTHIANS 2:14

"Aromatherapy" is a recent trend that teaches certain aromas can have powerful effects on our psyches. Commercials selling these aromas usually feature a woman relaxing in a bubble bath with her eyes closed and her head leaned back on a pillow. A peaceful smile graces the woman's face, which seems to float serenely on the cloud of bubbles billowing up under her chin. Just one whiff of this special fragrance, the ads seem to say, and you're twenty years younger, thirty pounds thinner, and forty times more likely to have Ed McMahon ring your doorbell and announce you've just won fifty million dollars.

In my case, any scents, therapeutic or not, detour through the kitchen before they reach my psyche. The truth is I have a hard time smelling anything—from flowers (which remind me of picnics in the park) to smoke (the signal in our home that dinner is done)—without having some image of food popping into my head. The pleasure I receive from thinking about food is second only to actually eating it. Just visualizing a hot fudge sundae or a succulent prime rib can send me drifting off to mindless bliss—and to the nearest restaurant! (As Bill says, "Barb cooks for fun, but for food, we go out!")

But all this "scent sense" is nothing new. Long ago, when I was in college, I waited tables in the campus dining room, which served big, fluffy, yeast-raised dinner rolls for Sunday dinner. Sitting in church on Sunday mornings, the aroma of those tantalizing dinner rolls would waft through the chapel windows, beckoning me to work (and to eat; we kitchen workers always sneaked a little "preview roll," just to make sure they were up to par). Like a shepherd's crook, the fragrance of that warm, flaky bread reached into the church pew every Sunday and pulled me out, toward the source of that wonderful smell.

"'Scuse me, 'scuse me," I would whisper as I scooted to the end of the pew and out the door. "I have to go to work."

Yes, indirectly at least, I'm as vulnerable to aromatherapy as anyone else—and have been for a long time. And there's one place where aromatherapy is really powerful, for me at least. I never really understood why until I read David Koenig's book *Mouse Tales* (Bonaventure Press, 1994), which shares some behind-the-scenes secrets about Disneyland, just a twenty-minute drive from our home in southern California. It turns out Walt Disney and his "imagineers" recognized the connection between scent and psyche long before the current aromatherapists made their discovery.

Whenever I walk down Main Street in Disneyland, I find myself smiling at everyone, even at that rambunctious family of twelve who cut me off at the entrance turnstiles a few minutes earlier. Before I know it, my mood has changed from harried tourist ready to rip the tires off the next baby stroller that runs over my toes to gracious guest sauntering jovially down the sidewalk on the verge of whistling "Zippity-Doo-Dah."

Part of the magical mood change comes from the subtle waves of scent that waft over the make-believe marketplace. From hidden vents in front of the Candy Palace comes the soothing scent of vanilla. At Christmas time, it's peppermint. And, I'm told, a couple of thousand miles away in Hershey, Pennsylvania, the same thing—only in wafts of chocolate—greets visitors to Chocolate World.

Fragrance can indeed be a powerful but invisible force, influencing more than just our taste buds. With the irresistible power of a tidal wave, it can sweep over us, changing what had seemed unchangeable: our attitudes.

God's Word is like that, too. It works its invisible power over us in ways that can be subtle or overwhelming. As C. S. Lewis said, it "whispers to us in our joys, speaks to us in our difficulties, and shouts to us in our pain." It changes our moods, reworks our attitudes, and infuses us with courage. We inhale God's love and exhale his goodness, breathe in his grace and breathe out his praise.

Like the woman in the bathtub, we soak ourselves in God's love, and it bubbles up around us, lifting our chins, soothing our spirits, easing our troubles, and bringing us peace in the midst of pain. It's the most effective therapy in the universe, and its fragrance clings to us wherever we go. We hope that others, passing through our lives, catch a whiff of God's love and find their attitudes changing and their hearts yearning for the Source.

"Gracious Lord, infuse me with the fragrance of your Word so that others sense in me the depth of your love and the joy of your presence. Amen."

FIRST IMPRESSIONS

Thelma Wells

Do not judge, or you too will be judged.

MATTHEW 7:1

Perhaps you've heard the expression, "You never have a second chance to make a first impression." It's true; the first impression is usually the lasting impression. But, thanks be to God, sometimes we get another chance.

When I met our friends James and Juanita Tennard, the scene was not pretty. It was about one in the morning. I was expecting our second child. I was fuming angry at my husband because he was out much later than usual. Because I was afraid something had happened to him, I was frustrated and angry.

When I saw the car come up the driveway, I met George at the door—and I didn't greet him with tender, loving care. I stormed at him, "Where have you been? What do you mean coming in here this time of night!"

He tried to explain. "I met my friends from Houston. We went out for dinner. They're in the car waiting to come in to spend the night. I told them you wouldn't mind."

Oh. Immediately, I turned my attention from fussing at him to inviting them into our home. Juanita says I said, "Come on in. Y'all are welcome. I'm not mad at you. I'm fussing at George." She said she was afraid to come in.

But once they got inside the house and I prepared a comfortable bed for them and shared with them my concern for George and why I was upset, they both understood. That fall night in 1963, even though I didn't make a very good first impression, an unwavering friendship began that has lasted over three decades through trials and hardships, good times and bad.

We are together several times during the year including Easter, weddings, anniversaries, graduations, births, and funerals. Their baby daughter, Tammy, started to walk in our living room.

James and Juanita's first impression of me was a mean, angry wife. Even though they remember that incident, they eventually got to know the real Thelma, and they gave me a second chance to create a more favorable impression.

I can't say I did the same during an incident that occurred in the mid-eighties. I walked into a Dallas bank to meet with an executive vice president about customer service training. I went up to the secretary's desk, smiled, and announced my name and my reason for being there. The secretary stopped working, looked me up and down, gave me no response, stood up, and walked off leaving me standing there. I was appalled. I assumed she had judged me and decided I wasn't worth a nod, grunt, or smirk let alone a smile or a handshake.

Looking for a friendly face, I found another worker and asked her to let the gentlemen know I was there. When I settled into a chair in the vice president's office, I started to tell him of the incident.

He cut me off and said, "What has she done this time?"

"This time! This time! Why is she here?" I asked.

The vice president explained that he often received complaints about her snippy behavior toward customers and coworkers, but he was hoping my seminar would help her to change. I didn't tell him I was no miracle worker, but that's what I was thinking. And even if I had been, I wouldn't want to ply my trade with her. I had no enthusiasm for Ms. Nose-in-the-Air's being in my class. My impression of that woman was set.

Well, surprise. When I taught the customer service class, she was a top participant. She was amiable, kind in her comments, pleasant, positive, polite, and poised. But none of that held any meaning for me. All I could remember was how ugly she had been toward me. I didn't know what caused her turnaround. Maybe she had been experiencing a lot of pain in her life.

Maybe I didn't have the full story. I didn't care. Nope, her lasting impression remained my first impression of her.

Now, I wasn't following Christ's admonition to give people room to make a second impression. I needed to give her a second chance. After all, that graciousness had been extended to me by James and Juanita—and Christ. That doesn't mean I would have changed my mind, but an entrenched attitude wasn't the way to approach the situation either.

Perhaps you have judged people without giving them a chance to show you who they really are. Maybe you have written a person off as someone you want nothing to do with. Maybe you have decided you can't work with someone on your team. Or maybe you refuse to work with a particular person on a committee at church. You may have even turned that person away from your home. That person just might deserve a second chance to make a first impression.

And how about you? How many times have you conveyed an impression to others you aren't proud of? How often do you wonder why you did or said something that caused another person to get the wrong impression? How often do you appear to be something you aren't?

When I create a wrong first impression, I'm consoled to realize God knows us inside out and outside in. He never has to wonder who we are or what we're up to. And if we behave badly sometimes, he understands what motivates us and accepts us even in our worst moments. I want to be able to do the same for others.

"Dear Lord, sometimes we act and perform in ways that send mixed messages about who we are. We've all made negative first impressions. Help us to be mindful of how we are to create, first and foremost, the impression of Christ's grace and mercy alive in us. Amen."

TREKKIN' DOWN THE ROAD

Potholes? What Potholes?

HORSIN' AROUND

Patsy Clairmont

His pleasure is not in the strength of the horse, nor his delight in the legs of a man; the LORD delights in those who fear him, who put their hope in his unfailing love.

PSALM 147:10–11

Hi-ho, Cecil. Away!

No, I didn't mean "Silver." Cecil is my horse. Well, I don't own her or anything. Actually, I've only ridden her once but she (or is it he?) is the only horse with whom I have stayed on speaking terms after a ride.

Here's the scoop (which, gratefully, I didn't have to use). I had been invited to visit Remuda Ranch, a facility in Wickenberg, Arizona, dedicated to helping young women with eating disorders. One of the perks of my tour was to be a horseback ride. My husband, Les, didn't think me wise to accept the invitation to ride the dusty trails. He wasn't worried about the dust, but he was worried about my rust—my rusty horse skills and my rusty body. And Les wasn't worried about the trail paths so much as he was my tailbone being splattered on the roadway. Oh, ye of little faith.

On my arrival Kay, my lovely hostess, greeted me with enthusiasm. We attended chapel services and then headed for the stables. My husband's cautions rang in my ears as I surveyed the saddled horses. I really had planned to just watch from the sidelines while the others rode until I spotted a particular horse.

I thought, *If I did agree to ride, that's the horse I would want*. He reminded me of my childhood days when I watched Roy, Dale, Trigger, and Buttercup on television every week. This horse looked like Trigger, and everyone knows Trigger would only take you on happy trails.

The playful staff encouraged me to ride along. I hesitated until Kay pointed to the horse (alias Trigger) and said he/she would be my steed. That was when I laced up my high-top riding boots and sauntered toward my horse. (Have you ever seen a five-foot person saunter?) The stable staff formally introduced the horse and me.

"Cecil? Cecil!" I repeated, shocked anyone would name Roy's horse Cecil. "Why, Cecil is a sea serpent."

But after they listed Cecil's calm virtues for the tenth time, I gave in and boarded my waiting transportation via a booster box. I assuaged my palpitating heart with the thought that Cecil was only a one-horse-power vehicle.

The six staff members, my daughter-in-law, Danya, and I lined up and headed out. Cecil and I moseyed along pretty well together. In fact, we were makin' tracks. The only challenge I had was my stirrups. They were a little too long for my short legs, and I felt like a toe dancer as I stretched to keep my feet in the stirrups (which had been hiked up as far as they would go).

Soon, as I was jostled to and fro in the saddle, I hit, you might say, my first pothole: My legs began to ache. But I continued on since we had only been riding three minutes. Well, about six minutes into the ride, my leg muscles began to scream, "Are you out of your mind? What do you think you're doing?!" Now my back (my second pothole) began to join in the whining chorus. Evidently my aerobic lifestyle of bench-pressing the newspaper and hoisting the mail had not prepared me for this equine workout.

Finally, with my legs stretched far beyond their designed reach and with a kink in my back the size of New Hampshire, I pleaded my cause with the staff. They immediately and compassionately headed for the stable. As I deboarded Cecil, after an eleven-minute ride, my legs wobbled. I looked like a Weeble as I toddled my way to a bench. For three days afterwards my back felt like Cecil had ridden me.

By the following morning, my wobbling was lessening, but my back continued to make threatening statements. I didn't mention this discomfort to my husband lest he feel, well, right or something.

Do you find it difficult to take good advice? To live within your limitations? To admit when you're wrong? Just remember, if you get a backache from carrying your horse, don't be surprised.

"Lord, may we not spend our life-efforts horsing around, but may we gallop toward wisdom. Amen."

I LIKE SMART WOMEN

Thelma Wells

When the queen of Sheba heard about the fame of Solomon and his relation to the name of the LORD, she came to test him with hard questions.

1 KINGS 10:1

One of my husband's favorite sayings comes from the television commercial in which a little child says, "I like smart women." When I say something he thinks is helpful, find something he has lost, or make a decision he thinks shows insight, he says, "I like smart women!"

A number of smart women show their stuff in the Bible. One of them is the powerful, beautiful queen of Sheba. Her wit, determination, leadership, negotiation skills, and willingness to learn about God fascinate me. Now, isn't that a list we'd all like to have appear behind our name in the Roster of Life?

The Arabian queen journeyed 1,400 miles to Jerusalem (we're probably talking camel here; for sure not a jet) to establish rapport with and learn from the wisest man who ever lived, King Solomon. I can just see them sitting down for dinner. She pulls out her pencil, licks its tip, and then flips open her steno pad filled with the questions she had thought up on that long journey. Her goal is to see what it would take to stymie this wise guy.

I can imagine her furiously penning Solomon's words and forgetting all about the Duck L'Orange on her plate. For he answered every question on her quiz to her satisfaction. (Why do I think she was a woman who didn't suffer fools?)

After the Q & A session, they moved on to a tour of his home. By the time Sheba had admired his well appointed palace, checked the end tables for dust and found none, noted that the waiters were elegantly dressed and hospitable while the cup bearers were solicitous, well, she was smitten.

Now, the queen was a woman of great possessions and influence herself, and she had multiple layers of reasons for the diplomatic visit to this king. She wanted to make a deal with Solomon, whose country lay between her land and the sea. She had in mind negotiating an international trade agreement. So she had packed in her luggage enticing gifts—gold, spices, and precious stones. Smart woman.

Ms. Sheba went back to Arabia with more than a trade agreement and a steno pad full of information. Her heart was touched by what she had learned of Solomon's God, and she returned to her realm to revolutionize the pagan religions. She introduced the idea of worshiping the true and living God to her people.

When I think about the Queen of Sheba and what she did for the world, I'm convinced that as fulfilling as having power, influence, possessions, education, commitment, and determination are, the most precious attribute in our lives is seeking and applying godly wisdom.

According to Proverbs, "The fear of the LORD is the beginning of wisdom" (Proverbs 9:10). Sheba feared (held in reverence) Solomon's God. As a matter of fact, she earned a commendation from Jesus himself when he said, "The Queen of the South will rise at the judgment with this generation and condemn it; for she came from the ends of the earth to listen to Solomon's wisdom, and now one greater than Solomon is here" (Matthew 12:42).

Have you discovered that the wiser we are the more successful we are in our endeavors? Our business thrives. Our personal and family relationships are intact. Our finances are under control. Our negotiations are fair. Our intellect is improved. Our spiritual lives are enhanced. Our Christian walk is easier.

I thank the Lord for the example of this smart woman who used her intelligence and spiritual openness to show the world that wisdom is the greatest attribute to seek.

"Father, sometimes we can think we're smart women until we find ourselves acting out of our own will without consulting you. When will we learn that wisdom only comes from you? Help us to lean on you as we conduct all of our affairs. Amen."

SING YOUR LUNGS OUT, YOU'RE FAMILY

Sheila Walsh

For I am convinced that neither death nor life, neither angels nor demons, neither the present nor the future, nor any powers, neither height nor depth, nor anything else in all creation, will be able to separate us from the love of God that is in Christ Jesus our Lord.

ROMANS 8:38–39

I love that my baby boy has no sense of what's appropriate on the noise-making front. He's as happy as a pig in mud and likes to share it with the world.

On the first Sunday we took him to church, we were nervous about leaving him in the nursery so we opted to sit in the back row, knowing that at the first squawk we could be up and out fast. He slept the whole way through the time of worship, the announcements, and the offering. We thought we were home free with a deeply spiritual child.

Then came the sermon. Christian was cuddled up in my arms, sucking his thumb, deep in sleep—or so I thought. Barry and I listened intently as our pastor talked about the shame that overcame King David when the depth of his sin rested upon him.

Suddenly, Christian burst into a baby version of "Moon River" at a decibel level that could have burst a dog's eardrums. I jumped up so quickly I nearly dropped him. Everyone turned to see whose baby was ruining the service. I hurried out whispering "Shh!" vainly in his ear. That only seemed to encourage him, and he moved into verse two, grinning from ear to ear.

By the time we were outside, I was laughing so hard I could barely walk or breathe. There is something so charming about that kind of innocence. When he is happy, we know it, and when he's not, we know that, too. It would never cross his mind to be anything but authentic.

When children are secure, they feel free to be who they really are. That's how you and I can live, too. God is the only one who knows everything about us. He knows our good thoughts and the thoughts that we struggle to admit even to ourselves. So no matter what you could tell someone else about your life that would change that person's opinion of you, nothing you could say would dampen God's heart toward you. He knows it all, and he loves you. Surely, this kind of security should set us free to be who we really are.

When we understand we aren't the hope or the joy but simply one who has been given the privilege of enjoying the one who is and passing his love on to others, life regains its spontaneity and laughter. I encourage you to meditate on God's words, "For I am convinced that neither death nor life, neither angels nor demons, neither the present nor the future, nor any powers, neither height nor depth, not anything else in all creation, will be able to separate us from the love of God that is in Christ Jesus our Lord" (Romans 8:38–39).

What a gift in a world where there is so much uncertainty! Why, it's enough to bring on a chorus of "Moon River."

"Lord Jesus Christ, I celebrate your love for me and in your presence sing. Hallelujah!"

JUST FOR FUN

Marilyn Meberg

For you make me glad by your deeds, O LORD; I sing for joy at the works of your hands.

PSALM 92:4

"Marilyn, how would you like to go to Antarctica for Christmas?" Luci asked as we made our way to the Palm Springs airport one day last summer.

Swerving the car slightly, I tactfully said, "I can't think of anything more unappealing! Why on earth would I want to go to Antarctica? Why would anyone want to go to Antarctica? Surely you don't want to go to Antarctica . . . do you?"

"It would be a fantastic way to see penguins in their natural habitat," she said cagily, knowing my affinity for penguins.

"But, Luci, I can go to Sea World if I need to see penguins! Besides, I'm a grandmother with two grandsons. You can't possibly think I'd miss Christmas with them to have Christmas with penguins. What in the world are you thinking?"

Knowing she had my full attention now, Luci told me she had been reading about a Straits of Magellan cruise that left from Valparaiso, Chile, rounded Cape Horn, and two weeks later concluded in Buenos Aires.

Puzzled, I said, "How does Antarctica and penguins fit into that?"

"Well, actually, that cruise is full, but this other cruise offers a flight over Antarctica for picture taking as well as a special road trip to Punta Tombo, the site of the largest Magellanic penguin rookery in the world."

Feeling slightly tricked, I nevertheless felt hooked as well. At the benevolent insistence of my kids, who reminded me that this was the year for the in-laws at Christmas, we all had Christmas together at Thanksgiving, and Luci, two other dear friends, and I flew to Chile. We boarded the ship December 13 and headed off for what proved to be an off-the-charts, fantastic trip.

The incomparable beauty of Chile astounded me as we moved slowly through the deep fjords, snow- and glacier-capped mountains, and photo-inspiring ice caps. Chilean scenery has to be one of the best-kept secrets in the world. Of course, it could well be that I was finally catching up with what the world has known all along.

By the time we rounded the Horn and headed for Puerto Madryn, I was really hyped. From there we would take a bus trip and travel one hundred miles south to the Magellanic penguin rookery. I'd never heard of this type of penguin (so what else is new?), but I learned they prefer warm weather, live in little dugouts, and sound like jackasses when they speak. I found all this information compelling, but I wasn't prepared for the utter delight I felt as our bus made its way down to the coastal rookery, carefully threading its way through hundreds of little penguins who didn't care whose parking lot they were on or how big our bus was. They had their own agendas, and we were not on it.

As we exited the bus, we stood literally knee-high in penguins. Some awkwardly headed for the ocean where they fell in while others milled about appearing to wonder what they should do next.

One particularly friendly penguin seemed to bond with our friend Mary as she leaned down and burbled and cooed in the love language reserved for her two little dogs. The wall-eyed penguin cocked her head to the far right and then to the far left in an apparent effort to comprehend what Mary was saying.

Then, seemingly bored, the penguin turned to the woman standing by Mary and began an energetic effort to loosen her shoelaces. When the shoelaces would not yield, the penguin pummeled the woman's leg with a succession of flipper slaps that sent us all into hysterics. With that, the penguin harrumphed off. The woman was not hurt, but she sported some memorable bruises the next day.

As we bused our way back to the ship, I felt content and grateful to God for the "works of his hands." To my knowledge, penguins don't serve any useful purpose in life other than to give people like me immense pleasure. Perhaps God put together some things in life for no other reason than that we might "sing for joy at the works of his hands." From the grandeur of the snow-capped glacier peaks to the awkward land inefficiency of penguins, what fun it is simply to "sing for joy" about his creation.

"Lord God, thank you for the immense beauty and diversity of your creation. Thank you for the opportunity to revel in it and to know from whom it came. Thank you that it delights your Father heart to give me, your child, joy. Amen."

MERE INCONVENIENCE OR MAJOR CATASTROPHE?

Luci Swindoll

The fear of the LORD leads to life:
Then one rests content, untouched by trouble.
PROVERBS 19:23

I found an article in the *London Times* that tells about a farmer's woeful day. Badly crushed under his tractor and temporarily blinded, he staggered home three-quarters of a mile then took off his boots to avoid dirtying the kitchen floor.

Fred Williamson had been using the headlights of the tractor for illumination while he repaired a water tank in the field. The hand brake failed, and the tractor ran over him, ripping his face with barbed wire caught in the tractor's wheels. Mr. Williamson suffered broken ribs and a collarbone, a punctured lung, and damage to his face that rendered him unrecognizable.

After the accident, he managed to turn off the tractor and close the gates behind him. He walked home and said to his wife, "Don't panic, Mary, but I need an ambulance." His jaw and cheekbones were broken, and his nose was in a thousand pieces. His left eye was missing. His wife said the first thing he asked her after his eight hours of surgery was if the water had been fixed.

Now, I have to admire that man. Of all people with a right to complain, Fred Williamson is one. However, I also have to laugh because Mr. Williamson took my philosophical approach to life to its extreme.

You see, when I hear people complaining, I often think, *They can't distinguish between a mere inconvenience and a major catastrophe*. We need to recognize the vast difference between the two. Nobody ever said life is easy, trouble free, or without problems. Everyone knows that. The secret to handling problems is how we view them. It's an attitude thing. Running out of coffee is inconvenient. A rained-out picnic is inconvenient. But a smashed jaw, broken cheekbone, crushed nose, and missing eye? We're talking catastrophe!

This past summer while traveling with a friend in the British Isles, we had a flat tire on our little rented car. Bummer! On a curve, a huge bus had taken its half of the road out of the middle, forcing us to run into a rock fence, flattening the tire, ruining the hubcap, and denting the fender. We managed to wobble the car down the road to a farmhouse, where we used the phone and waited for the repairman.

To some people this would have been a major catastrophe. After all, it wasn't our car, we were in a foreign country, we had no idea how much the repair would cost, and it took precious time out of our day. But that wasn't our feeling. While sitting on a rock waiting, we had a spectacular view of Ireland's coastline and plenty of laughter. Neither of us will ever forget the incident, and photos captured the memory.

Maybe I'm just a cockeyed optimist, but I think life is to be experienced joyfully rather than endured grudgingly. We know it brings complexities and trouble. Scripture affirms that. But why do we take minor irritations so seriously? Why do we act as though it's the end of the world? Think of the pain and conflict we would spare ourselves, the stress we would forego, if we just realized mere inconveniences can be survived.

This is all part of "resting content, untouched by trouble," as the verse for today describes it. It's believing when you trust God, regardless of the circumstances, you have "life, happiness, and protection from harm" (Proverbs 19:23 TLB).

The next time something gets you down and you want to whine or complain, remember Fred Williamson.

"Father, give us the grace to rest content in you no matter what. Teach us to trust. Amen."

ENCOURAGING WORDS

Barbara Johnson

Anxious hearts are very heavy but a word of encouragement does wonders!

PROVERBS 12:25 TLB

On that stormy night when the disciples saw Jesus walking on the water, they were scared out of their wits, thinking he was a ghost. But Jesus told them quietly, "Don't be afraid."

Peter, always the outspoken one, answered first. "Lord, if it's really you, tell me to come to you on the water." And Jesus said simply, "Come."

If you're a parent, you can probably remember when your children were first learning to walk. As they stood there, wobbling unsteadily, you probably said to them, ever so gently, "Come on. You can do it. Come on. Just try. Take a step."

Our arms outstretched, we coaxed and encouraged them. Eventually, believing our faith in them, they let go of the coffee table or Daddy's pant leg or the bathtub, and they took that first awesome step.

What wonders a bit of encouragement can do! It's one of the most awesome treasures God has given us—the ability to inspire, motivate, and reassure others.

Even babies have it. Scientists say a natural progression of infants' development is to learn to clap their hands together. That must mean God has given them a way to cheer on us parents (and God knows we need all the encouragement we can get!).

The apostle Paul reminded all of us, young and old alike, that if we've been given the gift of encouragement—and who of us hasn't at some time in our lives?—then we're to use it! (See Romans 12:8.)

Encouragement doesn't have to be profound. After all, Jesus encouraged the skeptical Peter to do the impossible with one little word: "Come." It just needs to be expressed.

Someone has said that encouragement is simply reminding a person of the "shoulders" he's standing on, the heritage he's been given. That's what happened when a young man, the son of a star baseball player, was drafted by one of the minor league teams. As hard as he tried, his first season was disappointing, and by mid-season he expected to be released any day.

The coaches were bewildered by his failure because he possessed all the characteristics of a superb athlete, but he couldn't seem to incorporate those advantages into a coordinated effort. He seemed to have become disconnected from his potential.

His future seemed darkest one day when he had already struck out his first time at bat. Then he stepped up to the batter's box again and quickly ran up two strikes. The catcher called a time-out and trotted to the pitcher's mound for a conference. While they were busy, the umpire, standing behind the plate, spoke casually to the boy.

Then play resumed, the next pitch was thrown—and the young man knocked it out of the park. That was the turning point. From then on, he played the game with a new confidence and power that quickly drew the attention of the parent team, and he was called up to the majors.

On the day he was leaving for the city, one of his coaches asked him what had caused such a turnaround. The young man replied it was the encouraging remark the umpire had made that day when his baseball career had seemed doomed.

"He told me I reminded him of all the times he had stood behind my dad in the batter's box," the boy explained. "He said I was holding the bat just the way Dad had held it. And he told me, 'I can see his genes in you; you have your father's arms.'

After that, whenever I swung the bat, I just imagined I was using Dad's arms instead of my own."

Like that young baseball player, we all have our heavenly Father's "genes." But sometimes we need to be reminded of the great potential we possess. We need someone to point out our likeness to the One who created us, to see God's image in us.

Just one little word of encouragement can make all the difference. Soon we're ready to step back up to the plate and take a swing at whatever life throws at us.

"Dear Lord, please give me the right words of encouragement to lift someone's heart today. Amen."

AH, SWEET REPOSE

Thelma Wells

Cast all your anxiety on him
because he cares for you.

I PETER 5:7

Sometimes, despite our best intentions, we find ourselves wandering in a wilderness of anxiety, lost and unable to find our way out. I know. For years I felt that way. Nothing seemed to work; I felt stripped and anxious, unable to determine what my mission in life should be. What was I aiming for? Where was a map out of this hazy land in which I wandered but couldn't find the path out?

It wasn't that I hadn't set goals. It's that I didn't know how to set my sights on God and let him lead me where to go. So, even when I was accomplishing what I had set out to do, I still felt lost.

Until one year when not only was I lost but I also lost everything. My business was at an all-time low, my husband had closed his business, and we had a small heap of money and a big mound of bills. Then I heard Dr. Charles Stanley of In Touch Ministries teach on anxiety. He said that the only way to get rid of anxiety was to humble yourself before the Lord and cast your cares on him.

For four days I thought about what he had said, wondering if it was that simple. By the fourth day, I was broken. I lay sobbing facedown on the floor in my bedroom. I remember praying, "Lord, I give my body, mind, soul, career, and family to you. I give you everything. Teach me your will. And I am determined not to get up from here until I feel some relief."

Much later, I woke up and discovered I was still on the floor. I had been in a deep, restful sleep. It must have been what the Bible calls "sweet sleep" because I awakened singing. I hadn't had a song in my heart for months. That was a turning point for me.

So it was no surprise when a couple of years later I was in a gathering with twenty-five well-established businesswomen. As we sat around chatting, drinking tea, and eating finger foods, one of them said, "Let's share our goals for next year." (The meeting was held toward the end of the year.) Each woman unfurled her major goal for the group:

"I'm going to expand my business into new areas."

"I will gross a half million next year."

"I want to add two new staff members."

"I just added a new administrator; now I can concentrate on starting another business."

"I plan to write my first book."

"I hope to take more time for my family."

"I'm going back to school."

Everyone had a goal. Finally, it was my turn. "I don't have any goals." The group looked puzzled. I'm sure most of them were thinking, *No goals? How can she be successful without goals?*

I continued, "I used to set goals all the time, but I've decided that wherever God leads me, I'll follow."

The room was quiet. I had been the last to speak. I'm sure a few ladies thought I was being irresponsible. But I didn't care. I had traveled through the wilderness of anxiety to come to this conclusion. Now, it's true that goals help us to be disciplined and to aim our energies toward accomplishing what we've set out to do. So goals in and of themselves aren't bad. But for me, setting goals and not leaning on God had led me into a perplexing and fretful place I didn't want to go back to. I had learned that first I needed to humbly go before God and give him my concerns. Then he will provide me with direction. But

the relinquishment and sweet repose were what I wanted to concentrate on since that day on the floor.

You may be in the same wilderness I was, anxiously wandering around, feeling aimless and without a map, fearful disaster is headed toward you. Relinquish your anxieties to God. For he cares for you. Directions will come in God's good time—and so will sweet sleep.

"Lord, teach me to come humbly before you, giving you all my concerns that weigh so much to me but are so light to you. I need you to lighten my load. Thank you for your gentle care for me. Amen."

FLIRTING WITH DANGER

Luci Swindoll

Charm is deceptive, and beauty is fleeting;
but a woman who fears the LORD is to be praised.

PROVERBS 31:30

My favorite place to travel is Africa. The place is filled with intrigue, risk, and adventure, but when one is on safari, the continent is even more fascinating.

The highlight of any safari is seeing a leopard. Most people never do. I know folks who have lived in East Africa for years but who have never seen this elusive animal. Nocturnal, solitary, and enormously independent, the leopard is also secretive and sensually seductive. Prowling the savanna by night, it silently stalks its prey, makes the kill, and hauls it into the limbs of a tree. All of which means the leopard is athletic, intelligent, and breathtakingly beautiful. An incomparable beast!

My friend Mary and I had been on a photographic safari for a week. We had not just seen but had studied the animals in their own environment. I had forty rolls of exposed film in my bag, and our journals were chockful of the splendor of our adventure. It had been perfect except for one thing: no leopard. Everyone told us that few were lucky enough to see the leopard. We shouldn't count on it.

Then, on the last day of our safari, as we were about to say good night to the African bush, we saw a gorgeous leopard strolling toward us with all the arrogance in the world. Our driver stopped. So did the leopard. He turned and sat upright next to us. He was posing. The setting added to the magnificence of the moment. It was like a George Innes painting. The dirt in that part of Kenya is a deep rust and rich with nutrients. The foliage was every shade of green, and the sky was comprised of gray, blue, and indigo. With this as his backdrop, the leopard sat in his slinky, spotted fur coat. His cold, intense, unblinking stare gave us goose bumps as we made eye contact with the beast.

After snapping three rolls of film, we reluctantly drove away. Almost immediately the driver stopped the truck and whispered casually, "Oh, theh is anotheh le-o-pard. You are veddy lucky with this miracle."

It wasn't luck at all. We had prayed to see a leopard. As we watched our second one in the same day, I relaxed and felt bold. He was so … close. So comfortable in our presence. So … charming. I wanted to reach out and pet him. I considered him a friend. I knew he was wild, but in that instant, he seemed tame.

How many times have you been in a similar situation? Something seems so innocent, so safe. You don't realize that what feels right has the potential to destroy. Scripture points this out in Proverbs 16:25, "There is a way that seems right to a man, but in the end it leads to death." It could be death of a relationship, finances, health, or life itself.

Predators are real. That's not a problem as long as we keep our distance. But when we drop our guard and feel comfortable, we are lured, then hooked, then devoured. We wonder how something so beautiful and charming could have been the messenger of death.

God's way of escape for his followers is to keep our eyes on the Lord, to fear and reverence him. Don't be enticed by a perfect setting, colorful surroundings, or beautiful creatures. The seductive predator might be lying in wait, ready to have you for lunch.

"Our loving, overseeing Father, keep us focused on you so we are not drawn away by that which breaks our hearts and our lives. Amen."

WHITTLING IN THE WOODS

Marilyn Meberg

That everyone may eat and drink, and find satisfaction in all his toil—this is the gift of God.

ECCLESIASTES 3:13

I've mentioned before that living in the desert is paradise. That is utterly true for about eight or nine months of the year. However, during June, July, August, and even into September, the word *hades* frequently comes to mind. Triple-digit temperatures that make a person dash from her air-conditioned home to her air-conditioned car characterize those months. But since everything here is of necessity air-conditioned, I don't think that our "I can't get outside" summer environment is any more troublesome than that of places where sleet, snow, and subzero temperatures limit outdoor activity. Every geographical location has its compensations as well as its challenges.

One of those summer compensations for me, an outdoor person, is the Palm Springs aerial tram that travels every twenty minutes to the top of one of our San Jacinto mountains. The mountain station is more than eight thousand feet up; so the minute I step out of the tram, I experience temperatures in the high seventies or low eighties. I also experience incomparable woodsy smells and the sound of tall trees allowing the breezes to glide through their branches. Those breezes caress my wrinkled face and lift my wilted spirits.

With my beach chair and book in hand, I find a spot under one of the many hospitable trees and settle in for a day in the woods. Once again I am in paradise.

One day last August, on a particularly hades-tinged day, I convinced my friend Pat to go up the tram with me. She was a bit hesitant because the vertical ascent up the mountainside in a tram seemingly suspended in midair was a bit daunting. Even though the tram information sheet stated four tract cables supported the tram, she still wondered if she might not be pushing God's inclination to "keep her from falling."

However, once safely up and settled under the protective cover of a grove of pine trees, Pat understood what I meant about reclaiming paradise. We read our respective books in companionable silence for a while, and then from her purse Pat pulled out a Swiss army knife complete with compass, scissors, screwdriver, and every other conceivable blade known to humankind. She began enthusiastically to whittle the bark off various dead branches strewn about our feet. This activity was accompanied by a tuneless whistling that began to threaten my state of paradise. Casting sidelong glances at her, I noted a look of absorption as well as delight. As she graduated from debarking small dead twigs to larger and larger branches, I finally asked her if she intended to build a little cabin.

Choosing to ignore the mild sarcasm in my question, she said, "Marilyn, I haven't done this since I was a kid; I am having so much fun!"

Up to the point of Pat's whistling I had been engaged in Philip Yancey's fantastic book, *What's So Amazing About Grace?* However, my mild annoyance with the increase of lumberjack sounds gave way to envy as I remembered idly and unskillfully whittling pieces of wood with my dad's jackknife while we waited for the trout to strike our fishing lines.

Laying Yancey facedown in the pine needles, I asked Pat if she needed to take a rest from her labors. If she did, I'd be happy to help her debark her latest dead branch. Smiling knowingly, she handed me her knife. That did it; I was snagged.

I don't know quite how to describe the feeling of utter contentment that came over me as I whittled and debarked away the next thirty minutes while Pat read Yancey. It was nostalgic, peaceful and—amazingly—spiritual. Odd as it may sound, I felt God smiling with me. After all, everything we were experiencing in that haven of wooded coolness was a gift from him: the air, the sounds, the contentment, and even the reflection on our childhoods had their source in God's divine plan.

Scripture says eating, drinking, and even toil are gifts from God. That experience in the woods was a wonderfully good gift. Of course, I went out the next day and bought myself a Swiss army knife. It even has a tiny saw! Now I'm ready for our next whittling time in the woods.

"I am surrounded by your many gifts, Lord, and I am grateful. Thank you for those gifts that restore my soul and my body. Thank you that all your gifts are available to me. Thank you that they are given out of the abundance of your Father love. Amen."

OFFSHOOT

Patsy Clairmont

He is like a tree planted by streams of water, which yields its fruit in season and whose leaf does not wither. Whatever he does prospers.

PSALM 1:3

I brake for trees. Yep, trees. I love all kinds—tall ones, squat ones, full ones, even skimpy ones. I, of course, enjoy trees that produce fruit, flowers, and colorful leaves. I also appreciate tree shade, tree shapes, and tree shadows. I even like tree droppings with the exception of black walnuts, which have an adverse effect on my flowerbeds.

Trees serve as a refuge for climbers, picnickers, tree houses, birds, squirrels, and nuts like me. I find most trees hospitable. In fact, my grandmother had a shade tree so generous it drenched her entire dwelling in soothing shadows, keeping her comfortable throughout the sultry Kentucky summers.

Some of my favorite trees are palm trees. They seem so perky even on their sassy hair (frond) days. That's not easy. When my fronds become unruly so does my 'tude.

The rough patterned bark of the palm interests me. Someone (guess who) spent a great deal of time designing the intricate detailing. When untended, some palms become untidy with dead fronds that look like my morning shredded wheat.

I also am enamored with weeping willows. They are so poetic. On breezy days they become lovely whisk brooms dusting the earth. On summer days their graceful branches lean toward the water's edge drinking in their environment. In a storm they become the eccentric scientist, wild with enthusiasm. And in the winter they take on a melancholy appearance, bowing low with grief.

Yes, yes, I love trees. Trees have inspired many poems. Why, even the village smithy wouldn't have wanted to bang hot iron without the protective covering of the spreading chestnut tree. And someone said he had never seen "a poem as lovely as a tree."

He must have been peering up a redwood. Those will cause one to pull off the road to take a closer gander. Imagine the toothpicks you could produce from one of those branches. I looked like a termite compared to that trunk—an undernourished termite at that. The redwoods cause people to hush and look up in awe. Hmm, maybe that was the idea.

When I was challenged years ago to select a life verse from Scripture, I headed for the trees. I chose Psalm 1:3 and the companion verse in Jeremiah 17:8. The Jeremiah passage compares a bush and a tree. Of course the tree wins. For the tree represents the righteous while the bush is a picture of those who put their trust in people instead of the Lord.

I guess with my five-foot stature I've always felt bush-like, and so my longing has been to grow into a rooted, shooted, fruited tree. (Tall isn't enough; I also want to be productive.) I am especially smitten with the fruit trees that grow in my own yard where I can be the benefactress of the apples and sweet cherries. And that premise carries over into my spiritual life as well. For as much as I love sharing my faith with others, the fruit is even sweeter when it benefits those who live in my own backyard.

What kind of tree are you? Are you planted near the water to avoid disaster should a drought occur? What type of fruit do you bear? Who is benefiting from your fruit?

"Lord, thank you for brake-screeching tree sightings that cause us to pull over. It helps us to slow down and admire your creativity. May we purpose to grow up into oaks of righteousness. And may we have the joy of watching our loved ones benefit from our shade and our fruitfulness because of your goodness. Amen."

WHO AM I?

Luci Swindoll

God said to Moses, "I AM WHO I AM."

EXODUS 3:14

But by the grace of God I am what I am.

I CORINTHIANS 15:10

I've never had an identity crisis. Nonetheless, I'm constantly clarifying who I am. The conversation goes like this:

"I love your husband. I listen to him on *Insight for Living.*"

"He's my brother."

"Aren't you his wife?"

"No, I'm his sister."

And then, with obvious disappointment and disillusionment, "But I thought you were his wife."

"No."

"Then the two of you aren't married?"

Finally, feeling sympathetic, I apologize. "I'm sorry. I'm not married to him."

With utter frustration, "But, why not? I told my friends you were his wife."

Please! I've often thought of wearing a sign, "No, I'm not his wife." I love the guy dearly, but I'm not married to him.

Not only do I experience this bit of confusion over my relationship to my brother, but there's also this voice of mine. It's always been low. My brothers used to tease me about being my own grandfather. As a voice major in college, I was contralto. In choirs, I choose the lowest harmonic note. But here's the most fun: in the wee morning hours, when I order breakfast in hotel rooms, they respond, "Yes, sir. Right away, sir." I play a little game with the phone. I look it squarely in the dial and say aloud, "It isn't 'sir.'" Even in Scotland, the operator said, "Aye . . . and we'll 'ave it right up to ya, laddie." It isn't "laddie."

I'm not "laddie," not "sir," not my own grandfather, and definitely not Chuck's wife. So who am I? Me. I'm myself. No other. No duplicate. No clone. Luci Swindoll—me.

Psalm 100:3 says, "Know that the LORD is God. It is he who made us, and we are his; we are his people, the sheep of his pasture." That pretty much settles it for me. Always has. He created me, and I'm who he wants me to be. Nothing more. Nothing less. Nothing else. That's true for you, as well.

The poet e. e. cummings wrote:

> To be nobody but yourself in a world which is doing its best, night and day, to make you everybody else—means to fight the hardest battle which any human being can fight; and never stop fighting.

I keep that in my address book as a reminder to be who I am, whom God made me.

The writer of Job says each of us has been uniquely shaped by God's hand. He has formed us exactly. The great I AM made us and shaped us. A blessed thought! I don't have to be anybody but me. And, as I walk with Christ, he's in the process of making me more like himself. God created us into who we are and "nothing is to be rejected" (1 Timothy 4:4).

Being who you are is sometimes difficult because you don't like who you are. Accept yourself as God's wonderful creation. Then you are free to be you without fear. I love hearing Sheila Walsh say again and again, "When someone asks me who I am, I say, 'I'm Sheila Walsh, the daughter of the King.'" Go, Sheila!

I've heard Chuck say repeatedly: "Sis, know yourself, be yourself, like yourself." Wise words.

Who are you? God's unique creation. There's nobody just like you. Never has been, never will be. Only you can be you. Be whom God made you.

"Father, we want to be comfortable with who we are. Work in us that we might be all you created us to be. Forgive us for rejecting your creation. Amen."

SNOOZIN'

Thelma Wells

Do not be afraid or discouraged, for the LORD God, my God, is with you. He will not fail you or forsake you.

I CHRONICLES 28:20

I don't know whether I'm getting old and forgetful or I'm just losing it. But I have evidence it's possible both are true. Two times recently I've missed events my heart was set on attending.

A couple of beautiful, intelligent young ladies who grew up in the church I attend set their educational goals and attained them. I was invited to the much deserved graduation and the everybody-will-be-there, after-graduation celebration. I was set to go!

On that particular Saturday I ran the usual errands and laid out my clothes for the graduation. Then I decided to take a fifteen-minute nap. I have a reputation around my house for being one of the world's fastest sleepers. Fifteen minutes of sleep rejuvenates me. So, I settled down for a quick nap. That little nap turned into eight hours of sleep.

I couldn't believe it. Obviously, I had missed the graduation and the celebration. I was heartsick! How could I explain to Geri, Ruby, and Earl that I slept through it all?

Now I better understand how Peter, James, and John felt when Jesus asked them to watch with him just one hour and those guys were caught napping. Their hearts probably dropped to the bottom of their stomachs, too. Not to mention their pulse rate increasing and their eyes becoming wide and watery. Their embarrassment was probably as visible as the wrinkles in their slept-in clothes.

Like me, the disciples probably started making a mental list of the ways they could have avoided missing one of the most important times in their friend's life. I thought that my story would have ended differently if I had sat in the chair and nodded; if I had fought the sleep and simply stayed awake; if I had asked someone to wake me up at a certain time.

All those ifs were too late. The damage was done. I had disappointed my friends and myself.

Then, I couldn't believe it, something similar happened during the Christmas holidays. Christi at New Life Clinics asked me to be the surprise guest for the employees at their annual Christmas dinner. I agreed. But I didn't write it down.

The day of the event, I was packing my office to move to another location. I kept feeling this annoying tug that said, "You're supposed to do something today." But I couldn't for all the moving boxes in Dallas think of what it was.

On Christmas Day someone asked me how the surprise appearance at New Life had gone. Oh, no! I felt "gone," all right. My heart was sick. As a matter of fact, every time I think of it even now, my stomach quivers, my heart beats faster, my head feels strained, and my body feels drained. I still want to kick myself.

Have you ever been in a similar situation? Did you face up to it (red-faced and all) and accept responsibility? Or did you avoid the issue and pretend it didn't happen?

Each time I forced myself to face up to what I had done. Telling the truth cleared my conscience and showed honesty. Everyone I had failed seemed to understand.

Wouldn't it be horrible if Jesus slept through some events in our lives? We would call him, but he couldn't hear the call because he was trying to rest. Wouldn't it be frightening to think he could forget our requests? Wouldn't it be tragic if he were so busy he couldn't remember what we talked to him about?

Thank God we don't have to endure that kind of treatment from our Lord! Psalm 121:4 says, "Indeed, he who watches over Israel will neither slumber nor sleep." It's consoling to know God not only doesn't sleep, but also he doesn't even get drowsy. We can depend on him to attend to our every need twenty-four hours a day, seven days a week. That gives us peace.

Isaiah 49:15 asks a poignant question about forgetfulness. "Can a mother forget the baby at her breast and have no compassion on the child she has borne? Though she may forget, I will not forget you!" Hallelujah, we are never forgotten! Even when our very own mother might not remember us, God can be depended on.

It's a bitter pill to think that we let others down. We disappoint loved ones. We inconvenience people we care about. But how wonderful, how beautiful, how comforting to know we have a God who is always near to console and cheer, just when we need him most.

"God of grace, thank you that we can depend on you to be available every minute of every day. Thank you that there are some things you can't do, like doze off or forget. Thank you that when we unintentionally disappoint our friends and loved ones, you give them a spirit of forgiveness. Amen."

ELEVATED

Patsy Clairmont

❖❤❖❤❖❤❖❤❖❤❖❤❖❤❖❤❖❤❖❤❖❤❖❤❖❤❖❤❖❤❖❤

I lift up my eyes to the hills.

PSALM 121:1

When I stepped into the hotel, I was dumbfounded to see columns of glass elevators cruisin' straight up the center of the open lobby from the first floor to the top floor. Faster than a speeding bullet, the cubicles shot up forty-seven floors—forty-seven floors! Did you hear me? Forty-seven! Why, I'm almost certain Jesus lives on the forty-eighth floor, or at least a band of angels. We're talking the heavenlies.

Our room was on the nineteenth floor—halfway to paradise. I stepped into the glass bubble and was instantly catapulted to the nineteenth level. Well, level was not what I felt as I stepped out on rubbery knees and wobbled my way to door number 1919.

My son Jason and his wife, Danya, later taunted me into peering over the guard rail and down into the lobby. Oh, gag, wrong move. My head felt unusually light (probably because I kissed my brains good-bye when I accepted their dare).

Jason and Danya seemed mesmerized by the view of the teensy-weensy people in the valley far below. Ah, sweet youth—where did mine fly away to? (It's probably soaring with my brains on level forty-eight.)

At one point during my stay, I had to travel to the fortieth floor for a meeting. I'm certain on the way up we passed through a layer of cumulus clouds. My host served hors d'oeuvres, but I preferred oxygen. I discovered the music I was hearing in the background was actually my ears' rhythmic popping as they tried to equalize the pressure.

For me, height is pressure. I wonder if that's why God designed me with such a limited stature (five foot). He knew I couldn't handle the altitude. As sensitive as I am to heights, I'm afraid if I were very tall I'd experience one constant nosebleed.

Les and I spent part of a winter in the desert in California. We resided in a basin surrounded by mountains. Now, even though basin sounds as if I could be rinsed (or flushed) down the drain, somehow that is more comforting to me than to risk stepping off a cliff. Know what I mean?

Also my joy is increased when I follow the psalmist's example. "I lift up my eyes to the hills." Notice he doesn't say, "I lift up my body to scale those hills."

Of course, the Bible does recount a few times in which the Lord required his people to climb to scary heights. Like Moses when he made the trek up Mt. Nebo. I've often wondered how difficult Moses found it to leave his brother, Aaron, at the base of the mountain while Moses went on alone.

I believe the more people involved the less scary, as well as the more the merrier. Although going with me to heights is like taking along your own tourniquet. My vice grip on your arm will tighten significantly with each uplifted step we take together.

Actually, when you think about it, many scary steps are required right here on ground level that help us reach new heights. Hmm. Remember when Zacchaeus came down from his pompous perch and responded to the call of the Lord? That was when he began to grow up. That means sometimes down is up and up is down. Uh-oh, this sounds like a merry-go-round. (I don't do them either.)

I have learned that uppity is a downer, for we are warned about being high-minded, that is, thinking more highly of ourselves than we should. (Watch out, a pothole!) Like the time I thought I was lookin' good only to discover my pantyhose were underfoot—or more accurately, they were streaming behind my foot as I sashayed through the middle of town. Not a pretty sight.

In fact, when we use items outside of their designed purposes, we often encounter problems. Pantyhose are better utilized under our clothing rather than trailing behind us for public viewing.

Remember in Genesis when Joseph paraded his new coat for his brothers' viewing? They, in turn, stripped him of his colors and sold him into slavery. Yep, showing off (pothole!) tends to trip us up. Joseph spent a lot of years behind bars for seeing stars—his being the brightest one of the bunch. Thinking more highly of ourselves than we ought means a downfall is probably up ahead. I guess God knew for Joseph to grow up, he would have to live down his need to be the center of attention. Here, though, is the amazing truth: Joseph grew to handle his down times as well as he did his up times. He became an example to many as his social position looked an awful lot like a busy elevator.

The elevators at the hotel I stayed in were the central focus of the lobby. The glass cubicles were studded on the outside with lights, which made them lovely to watch ascend and descend. People sat and studied those moving booths glide effortlessly from the first floor to the top floor.

Which leads me to ask, Who is the central focus of our lives? The Lord? Or our need to be center stage? Are we willing, whether we ascend or descend, to be a shining example? And, finally, does our elevator go to the top floor?

"Lord, may you be high and lifted up in our lives. Amen."

MILES OF SMILES

The Joys of Good Car Companions

DRUNK WITHOUT DRINKING

Barbara Johnson

Dear friends, since God so loved us,
we also ought to love one another.

1 JOHN 4:11

When I was preparing to undergo some minor surgery recently, the doctor warned me the anesthesia might make me a little goofy even hours after the surgery was completed. For a moment I wondered whether anyone who knew me and thought I was already pretty goofy would even notice. Then I remembered that it's my husband, Bill, who's the peculiar one, being an only child and all.

The doctor said that, when I left the hospital, I was not to drive a car, sign any contracts, or make any irrevocable decisions because I would be considered legally drunk for twenty-four hours after the surgery. Never having had a drink of alcohol in my life, I had no idea what to expect. *Just think,* I told myself, *you're gonna be drunk without even taking a drink!*

The idea was so amazing to me that I started imagining I was drunk even before the surgery started. When I arrived at the outpatient desk, the receptionist shoved a stack of papers toward me and told me to "fill them out, check the things that apply, and then sign here, here, and here. Be sure to press hard, because it's a triplicate form."

In my imaginary state of drunkenness, I had a little trouble following her rapid-fire instructions, but I finally completed them all. In just a moment the door opened, and a nurse called me in. As soon as she had me settled in a bed, three other nurses slipped through the curtain.

"Oh, Mrs. Johnson," one of them said in a low, excited voice, "we're so thrilled to have you here. When we saw your name on the admittance forms and realized it was you, we called you back early. All of us have read your books. I even have one of them here, and I was hoping you would sign it for me."

I wanted to beg off, pleading imaginary drunkenness, but since she was a nurse she would know I hadn't had any anesthesia yet. So I signed her book and then looked at the four of them expectantly, wondering what would happen next.

They stood around my bed, their faces glowing with friendly smiles. Suddenly my little cubicle had taken on a party atmosphere. I wondered if it was because I was drunk—and then I remembered I wasn't, at least not yet.

"Barb, could we pray with you before your surgery?" one of the nurses said. Enthusiastically, the four of them joined hands, and the two nearest me clasped my hands in their own, and they prayed the sweetest prayer I'd ever heard. (Of course I thought I was inebriated, so just about everything was sounding pretty good to me then!)

Outside the curtain, I heard a man clear his throat. "Oh, Dr. Brown!" one of the nurses said, peeking out of the curtain. "We're just saying a little prayer for Barb. Would you mind waiting a minute?"

Evidently he agreed, because she returned and the prayer continued.

In just a moment the nurses' prayers ended, and the anesthesiologist stepped up to my bed and gave me a reassuring pat on the arm. He, too, said a little prayer, asking God to be with all of us in that operating room. Under ordinary circumstances I might have become a little apprehensive, knowing the moment had come for the surgery to commence. But he held my hand, and in my imaginary drunkenness—and having just heard the nurses pray for me so thoughtfully and sincerely—I managed to flash him a smile before the lights went out . . .

To be honest, I don't think I was ever "drunk" during those twenty-four hours after my surgery, but I certainly was on a high. I kept remembering those thoughtful nurses and how they had surrounded me with their love and held my hands in theirs—and then sent me off to La-La Land with their prayers echoing through my mind and filling my heart with peace. The joy that memory brought me erased any discomfort the minor surgery might have caused.

By that evening, I was feeling fine—and even a little mischievous. Knowing Bill had been warned by the doctor to beware of my expected intoxication, I could tell he was constantly watching me out of the corner of his eye. For just a moment, I was tempted to put a lampshade on my head and dance a jig on the sidewalk then call up a real estate agent and sell the house. But just imagining how startled Bill would be was enough fun. And besides, being peculiar is his job.

"Dear Father, we are so grateful to you for sending your representatives into our lives to hold our hands and pray for us when fear threatens our peace. Your love is intoxicating, Lord! It heals us, sustains us, and fills our lives with joy. Thank you! Amen."

TWO ARE BETTER THAN ONE

Luci Swindoll

Two are better than one, because they have a good return for their work: If one falls down, his friend can help him up.

ECCLESIASTES 4:9–10

Sometimes I think I'm the Lone Ranger. I'm the picture of solitude and independence. I entertain myself for days with no help from anyone.

But that isn't always the case. Every now and then I feel the need for connectedness. I want to be surrounded by my circle of friends. Being alone just doesn't cut it. That's what happened last summer when I started out thinking I was the Lone Ranger.

I was in Ireland with a friend. On the day we were scheduled to fly to Scotland, I awakened feeling ill, chilled and nauseated. My friend suggested we reschedule our flight, but I insisted I'd be fine. I fully intended to rise up and walk, to get myself packed, dressed, to the airport, and on to the next country on our itinerary. I was sure I wouldn't need any help, being the Lone Ranger and all.... In the meantime, I went back to bed.

When I awakened from my feverish stupor, my traveling companion had gathered up my things, packed my bags, and made all the arrangements for us to leave. She asked again if I wanted to delay our departure. Of course not! I insisted I'd be fine. The minute we climbed in the cab, I fell sound asleep.

Arriving at the airport, again I heard, "Do you want to leave later?" Of course not! I insisted I'd be fine. So while I rested in a wheelchair inside the terminal, she stood in line, checked in our bags, and collected our boarding passes. I fell fast asleep in the chair.

This went on all day, with my insisting I could make it on my own while she did both my part and hers. I fell asleep every time I found a place to sit.

Ultimately, we arrived at the hotel in Scotland. While she made sure our possessions were brought to the room, found a drugstore, and bought medicine, I crawled into bed.

It wasn't until the next day I figured out how I got there. I had had a caretaker in my time of need . . . one who joyfully provided for me when I was oblivious to her acts of kindness and hard work.

That's the way life is, isn't it? We need each other. Scripture says two are better than one. We're instructed to love, pray for, care about, accept, forgive, serve, encourage, and build up one another.

I love that about my partners in the Joyful Journey conferences. We bebop all over the country watching out for each other. We serve one another joyfully, from the heart. When one of us is down, we rally to her. When one celebrates, we rejoice together. We're a team. We never anticipated this kind of bonding, but bonded we are.

People need each other—no matter how much we insist we don't. Nobody is an island, an entity unto herself, or a Lone Ranger. We're in this thing called *community*, and part of the joy of community is sharing the weight. The weight of burdens, losses, loneliness, and fear.

Look around you, my friend. Who's there for you? And who are you there for? Take a careful look. Even those who insist they can make it on their own may just be waiting for you to reach out and help. Be there and available. Even the Lone Ranger had a sidekick.

"Father, thank you we are not alone. You are with us. Always. And you give us the gift of friendship. Don't let us miss the joy of it. Amen."

TRAVELING CHUMS

Patsy Clairmont

A friend loves at all times.

PROVERBS 17:17

Choosing the companions who ride in your car can be great fun. I remember in high school gym class, when I was selected to be on a team, I was exuberant. That is, if I were selected early on and not as a last-ditch choice. I was often last pick in my neighborhood because the baseball teams were mostly boys, and they didn't want an ol' girl.

Well, today this ol' girl is enjoying miles of smiles with the Joyful Journey team. And given first dibs on travel companions, I would pick Thelma, Luci, Marilyn, Sheila, and Barbara right off the bat. These ladies hit home runs repeatedly. Let me tell you how.

Thelma is an honorable woman of the Word. I love to observe Thelma as she delves into the Scriptures. I can always tell when she has just read something that has struck a chord in her heart. She will whisper, "Yes, Lord, yes. Thank you, Jesus." Thelma often is tucked in a corner behind the scenes, Bible spread open, preparing herself for ministry. Thank you, friend, for being an example of one who stays current in the Word. Thelma, because you have studied the Map, I pick you to point the way on our trip.

I want my humorous companion Luci to be the tour guide. She always seems to know where to stop and what to do to have an uproarious time. And Luci can guide us into stimulating conversations as well with her witty, thought-provoking questions. She often causes me to think more deeply and explore more widely. Luci has helped me capture the bigger picture along my journey.

Now, Marilyn is our wholesome entertainment committee. Her infectious joy, fun-loving nature, and outrageous view of life qualify her for this task. Marilyn makes friends faster than anyone I know. She immediately embraces people with acceptance and laughter. And she keeps us all chortling and challenged with her comedic sense and her insightful offerings.

I'm putting Sheila in charge of music for the journey. Not only because she has a lovely voice but also because she has a lovely heart, one filled with God's light. Sheila's determination to be authentic is admirable and exemplary. Her brilliant mind, lightning humor, and sterling devotion cause my heart to sing, "Oh, Lord, how great thou art." Sheila's honesty brightens my path.

Barbara longs to be helpful so she, if you haven't figured it out, is our driver. (The girls won't let me drive because my foot doesn't reach the pedal. Or did they say it was because my elevator doesn't go to the top floor?) Barbara is the Joyful Journey senior team player. She is experienced in swerving to miss potholes and wheeling around big rigs, and she regularly brakes for joy. Her road has not been easy, but her faith has kept her on course. She is a seasoned journeyer who has taught me how to travel on with smiles in my miles.

The team suggested for our journey I could either sit on the hump in the middle of the back seat or in the trunk. I choose the hump, which puts me between Sheila and Marilyn—they tend to get rowdy when in proximity to each other. If they act up too much I may switch to the trunk.

Who are your traveling chums? Do they promote smiles in your miles? Do they help you miss unnecessary potholes? Do they add joy to your journey?

Joyful Journey girls, get in the car! Watch out, world, six outrageous women are heading down life's highway on a mission of joy.

"Lord, when we choose up teams, may we be wise and select traveling companions who are wholesome, humorous, helpful, and honorable. And remind us, Lord, to regularly brake for joy. Amen."

WHEREVER I AM

Marilyn Meberg

My purpose is that they may be encouraged in heart and united in love.

COLOSSIANS 2:2

I love the word *fellowship*. It connotes warm and chatty dinner parties, great walks on the beach, or sitting with someone significant in front of the fire drinking tea and sharing souls.

The Greek word *koinonia* is used in Scripture for our word *fellowship* and is defined as "that which is in common." *The International Dictionary of the Bible* defines *fellowship* as "that heavenly love that fills the hearts of believers one for another and for God. This fellowship is deeper and more satisfying than any mere human love whether social, parental, conjugal, or other." I love that definition, and of course, when I say I love the word *fellowship*, what I really love is the experience of fellowship.

I was so aware of the lack of fellowship potential among other shipboard persons on a South American cruise I took this past Christmas. On the ship were 1,200 people, many of whom I assumed were attempting to escape holiday-induced pain. But it lives within and schleps along with us even through the Straits of Magellan. I noted at times a poignant sadness that seemed to play across the faces of so many of my fellow passengers. Many seemed reluctant to socialize, and when they did, they lacked enthusiasm.

In contrast, my three traveling friends, whom I have known and loved for more than twenty years, and I daily experienced with each other the "heavenly love that fills the hearts of believers one for another and for God." Especially rich in fellowship was Christmas day.

Since it was the first Christmas I hadn't been with my grown children, I assumed I'd be swallowing lumps all day and talking to myself about the value of "letting go" and all that baloney. Instead, we four gathered in Luci Swindoll's room, where she had set up a little Christmas tree she had made with children's blocks and decorated with tiny toys she had glued to the blocks. We listened to Christmas music on the portable CD player Mary Graham had stuffed in her luggage, read Scripture, and prayed together. Then we exchanged gifts.

What fabulous Christmas fellowship! It was so deep, so sweet, and so Jesus-centered, it went far beyond the beautiful ship decorations, ship food, and the crew members singing Christmas carols in the ballroom.

However, the ultimate experience of Christian fellowship occurred the day after we disembarked and settled into our hotel rooms in Buenos Aires. Because Luci's brother Orville had pastored for so many years in Buenos Aires, we were eager to attend the church he had planted, watered, and fed. Though he now lives in Miami, he had arranged for the four of us to be taken to the church Sunday morning for the service.

Before we even entered the building, the spirited sounds of singing and clapping met us on the sidewalk, enveloped us, and literally propelled us forward. We were surrounded by radiantly smiling Latin faces singing praises to God with utter abandon. For a number of minutes I could only cry.

Not only was I moved by the powerful presence of the Holy Spirit in that place, but I also realized how rejuvenated I felt to be enveloped by believers. After two weeks on a ship where the majority of passengers were not spiritually inclined, it felt wonderful to be bathed in the oneness of these dear Christians who hugged and kissed us with such unaffected genuineness. That sweet Sunday will live forever in my memory as I reflect on fellowship that was unhindered by language or cultural barriers.

I'm convinced that wherever I am—on a ship in South America, in a church in Buenos Aires, or in my hometown of Palm Desert, Christian fellowship is mandatory for my heart and soul. Nothing can take its place.

How about you? Are you pining for the fellowship that surpasses all others? Get yourself to the nearest Christian and connect. Spend time with fellow believers rejoicing over what you have in Jesus. Sing some songs. Laugh together. Pray for one another. Hug each other. Celebrate the blessed tie that binds you to one another in Christian love.

"Thank you, Father, for the God-infused kinship that makes Christian fellowship so fulfilling. Thank you for the indwelling presence of your Spirit that unites our hearts and draws us together. May we reach out to each other, receive each other, love each other, and rest in each other. Thank you for the sweet experience of fellowship that rests on the sure foundation of who you are. Amen."

WHAT'S UNDER YOUR HOOD?

Sheila Walsh

When they saw the courage of Peter and John
and realized that they were unschooled, ordinary men,
they were astonished and they took note
that these men had been with Jesus.

ACTS 4:13

"I didn't know I had it in me," my friend said as we both collapsed into our seats on the bus. "I haven't run that hard in a long time. I guess there's life under the hood yet!" We both laughed as we gasped for breath.

Do you ever wonder what's under your hood? I don't mean the ability to run a mile in less than four hours, but the real stuff, the stuff of life. Stuff like courage—and fear.

Those two attributes are strange bedmates. It would seem impossible to experience both of them at the same time, yet I believe that's the challenge of the Christian life. Fear tells us that life is unpredictable, anything can happen, but faith replies quietly, "Yes, but God is in control."

If we will stop for a moment during our cluttered lives to reflect, we will realize this life is not a rehearsal. This is it. How will we choose to live?

I want to live a passionate life. I want to live a life that recognizes the fears but moves out with courage. I want to show the world the eternal mystery of what God can do through a miserable sinner sold out to him. Why would I settle for anything less? I've certainly had a life of courage modeled for me by several people in my life.

During a Women of Faith conference, Luci Swindoll asked me to stop by her room because she had a gift for me. Knowing Luci, there was no telling what it might be: a balloon, a puppy, two orphans from Kenya! This time it was a book of poetry and one poem in particular.

"Sit down," she said. "I want to read this to you if I can without crying." The poem, by Edna St. Vincent Millay, is called "Courage." Let me share an excerpt.

The courage that my mother had
Went with her and is with her still: . . .
Oh, if instead she'd left to me
The thing she took into the grave!—
That courage like a rock, which she
has no more need of, and I have.

Luci and I sat for a few moments with tears rolling down our cheeks as we voiced silent prayers of gratitude to God for our mothers. Luci's, who has gone to be with Jesus, and mine, who is still with me.

I see courage and fear mixed together in my friends, in women of faith, too. Barbara Johnson is a visible testament to Christ and to courage. She has been sideswiped by more sadness than a roomful of women has experienced. Yet her head is held high, and her gaze is fixed. It's fixed on Jesus.

Every woman who comes to our conferences wishes that Luci were her sister, her buddy. She loves life. She doesn't play it safe. She shows up soaked to the skin in the grace and mercy of God because she takes risks, she loves lavishly, she purrs like the only cat in the building who knows where the cream is.

Marilyn Meberg puts flesh onto the bones of what it means to die every day to self. She gives us a picture of her heart. We all see it. It's a heart with a zipper down the middle, and she chooses and chooses and chooses to live out of the half that loves God more than she loves herself.

Patsy Clairmont makes us laugh till our sides ache, and into that palace of joy she gifts each one of us with nuggets of truth. She tells us that, when it seems as if our path took a wrong turn, we should take a second look. In that diversion is a gift of grace.

Thelma Wells is honest, vulnerable, encouraging, warm, hopeful, and joyful. Her life tells us why we need to live a combination of fear and courage: "Life is tough, but God is faithful."

What a privilege to travel with women like these. But I'll let you in on a secret: You're a woman like this! All the things that rest within my dear friends resides in you. All you have to do is gather up your soul and determine that in Christ you will be a woman of courage, a woman of conviction, a woman in control of her fear, a woman of faith. Check under your hood. It's all there—in Christ.

"Thank you, Father, for all you have given me in Christ. I choose to be a woman of conviction and courage, of faith and hope, of love and life, in Jesus' name. Amen."

KEEP PATCHING

Luci Swindoll

Now we ask you, brothers, to respect those who work hard among you, who are over you in the Lord and who admonish you. Hold them in the highest regard in love because of their work.

1 THESSALONIANS 5:12–13

Seven years ago I read an article in the *Los Angeles Times* that I kept. It's about a graduate of Whitworth College who anonymously provided seventeen faculty members with vacations, gifts, and various gestures of kindness to say thanks for an education that changed his life. One teacher, on returning from a trip to Hawaii, said, "I look for ways now to express my own generosity." The whole idea had a ricochet effect.

Last night I finished reading a book, *Tuesdays with Morrie*, written as a tribute to a teacher. The author tells of the life-changing lessons he learned from his old Brandeis University prof, Morrie Schwartz, who was on his deathbed. Every Tuesday for fourteen weeks the former student, Mitch Albom, went to Morrie's home, where they discussed the world, family, emotions, money, the fear of aging, and forgiveness. Each Tuesday Mitch learned words of wisdom, encouragement, and love, imparted by an old man to his young friend.

It reminded me of my favorite teacher, Florence Bergendahl, or Bergie, as we called her. What a character! She was tall, with a majestic presence, perfect posture, a purposeful stride, and booming voice. She barked out pet phrases and short homilies: "Straighten up . . . never slouch . . . a good soloist stands tall and gets down to business. Remember your voice is *you*, so speak up . . . sing up . . . let us hear *you* behind that sound box."

On Saturday afternoons Bergie turned up the Metropolitan Opera broadcast full blast as she putted golf balls down the hallway of the teacher's dorm. When that little ball entered the tilted cup at the far end, she would gleefully laugh and, with full voice, sing along with the radio.

I studied voice with Bergie, but from her I learned some of life's greatest lessons. We discussed music, art, travel, lifestyles, books, learning, loving, and losing. She once said to me, "Life is like a patchwork quilt with joys and sorrows, gains and losses, fullness and hunger, and until you die, you'll keep patching. This is what gives meaning to life."

I loved her dearly, and when I sing, I think of her and her profound investment in my life. Every note that comes from my mouth is a thanks for what she gave me.

Sometimes I wonder if we've lost the art of expressing gratitude. We miss the joy of verbalizing appreciation, and we rob others of the joy of hearing how grateful we are. We don't know what to say or do.

As today's Scripture points out, we should respect those who have worked hard among us. Give back—not necessarily a plane ticket to a foreign country or a published manuscript, but something to reflect the value of the investment made . . . and something from the heart. That's when the giving continues. Someone gives to us . . . we give to another . . . they, to another . . . and on it goes. As Barbara Johnson says, it's boomerang joy bursting out all over.

Mitch Albom ends his tribute to Morrie with these questions: "Have you ever really had a teacher? One who saw you as a raw but precious thing, a jewel that, with wisdom, could be polished to a proud shine?"*

---

*Mitch Albom, *Tuesdays with Morrie* (New York: Doubleday, 1997), 192.

Does someone come to mind? Ask the Lord to give you a creative way to thank that person for his or her gift to you. "Hold them in the highest regard in love because of their work."

"Lord Jesus, our greatest teacher, instruct us how to express our appreciation to those who have labored hard, helping us to grow. Amen."

DADDY HARRELL AND THE PRAYER MEETIN'

Thelma Wells

. . . Who wants all men to be saved and to come to a knowledge of the truth.

I TIMOTHY 2:4

In God's infinite plan for my life, he allowed me to be born out of wedlock to a crippled girl whose parents were so embarrassed by the situation they forced her to leave their home and find her own way. When I was about two years old, my mother and I both became very ill. Granny, my great-grandmother, convinced my mother to let me live at Granny's house so she could nurse me back to health. During my convalescence, Granny and my great-grandfather, Daddy Harrell, became very attached to me. So, when my mother got well, the decision was made to allow me to stay with my great-grandparents. Granny always told me that my mother didn't give me away, she just let them keep me while she worked and tried to make it on her own.

Daddy Harrell and I became best friends. He was blind, but as soon as I was old enough to learn my way around the neighborhood, I became his eyes. I held his hand and led him down the street to Taplett's Fish Market, to the doctor's office, to visit his friends, or to church.

One of our favorite after-school games was "prayer meeting." The little parlor of our garage apartment became the St. John Missionary Baptist Church. The old sofa was the pew, and a tall-backed chair was the pulpit. Together, Daddy Harrell and I sang the old, metered hymns of the church and hollered out long-winded prayers, the kind late-arriving church attendees hated because it would be so long before the praying ended and they were allowed to be seated.

I remember some of them saying, "Honey, you better get inside the church before Daddy Harrell starts praying. You know he don't know how to stop once he gets wound up."

Daddy Harrell sang with more enthusiasm than talent, but he could remember every word of his two favorite hymns, "When the Battle Is Over We Shall Wear a Crown" and "I Shall Not Be Moved." His slightly off-key baritone wavered alongside my loud, childish voice. Together we belted out songs and prayed down fire and brimstone in our make-believe church.

When I think of Daddy Harrell, I feel love all over. His tolerance, patience, and most importantly, his presence was like that of God. I know my heavenly Father because I have seen him in the people I love.

God knew my great-grandparents' nurturing would be the catalyst that would propel me to learn the truths about who God was and how he works in our everyday lives. And those play prayer meetings would be so engraved in my heart I would transfer praying into a lifelong activity and into the lives of my children and grandchildren.

Through the examples of my Granny and Daddy Harrell, I would internalize the power of the names of God. In my prayer time I can call him:

Jehovah Yahweh (I Am Who I Am)
Jehovah Jireh (The Lord Will Provide)
Jehovah Nissi (The Lord Is My Banner)
Jehovah Shalom (The Lord Is Peace)
Jehovah Shammah (The Lord Is There)
Jehovah Tsebaoth (The Lord of Hosts)
Jehovah Elohe Israie (The Lord God of Israel)
Jehovah Rapha (The Lord God Has Healed)

Just as Daddy Harrell trusted me to lead him from place to place without fear of falling or being run over by a car, he taught me to trust God by turning over to him my fears and anxieties. Daddy Harrell's eyesight prevented him from reading, but he had memorized some Scripture while he still had sight. His remedy for my fear was Psalm 23:4, "Even though I walk through the valley of the shadow of death, I will fear no evil, for you are with me; your rod and your staff, they comfort me." He recited that verse to me often.

Perhaps you've had somebody who lived before you the truth of God. Cherish the memories and apply the truths. Maybe you haven't. But you can become that person to someone you care about. You don't have to play at pretend prayer meetings; all you have to do is live your life of faith for your loved ones to see. Take them by the hand and lead them to spiritual safety.

"Jehovah, I'm glad I know you are the Creator. Jesus, I'm glad I know you are my Savior. Holy Spirit, I'm glad I know you are my Comforter. For those I love who do not know these truths, I pray for their awakening. And I ask you what part you would have me take in waking them up. Amen."

WHERE'D YOU GET THOSE EYES?

Barbara Johnson

Who gives [you] sight or makes [you] blind? Is it not I, the LORD? Now go; I will help you.

EXODUS 4:11–12

Robb R. Hicks is not only a gifted ophthalmologist, but he's also a compassionate Christian man. I look forward to my checkups, knowing he'll always share some tidbit that will add a splash of joy to my day.

In his practice, he sees the human eye's amazing intricacies, and he helps his patients understand the great gift God has given them. His medical focus may be ophthalmology, but in layman's terms, he's an encouragement specialist. If it's true that the best exercise for the heart is reaching down and lifting someone up, Dr. Hicks's heart must be a perfect example of fitness.

Sometimes the diagnoses he must share are heartbreaking. But when this kind of news must be delivered, you won't find Dr. Hicks standing in the doorway, anxious to leave. He doesn't announce his findings in cold, professional terms to the family huddled around their loved one's bedside. Dr. Hicks discovered long ago that when you share someone's joy, it doubles; when you share someone's grief, each tear is divided in half. So he shares the grief his patients feel, often with tears in his own eyes as he tells them a deteriorating condition or a devastating injury is irreversible.

He's told me how he came to feel comfortable with this sharing of his emotions. Several years ago, when he had to tell some distraught parents and grandparents that one of their beautiful, two-year-old daughter's eyes would have to be removed because of cancer, he went to their room, planning to be an example of self-discipline so that they might gain strength from his controlled demeanor.

Instead, as he sat and talked with the sobbing parents, holding their hands, Dr. Hicks said, "I began to weep, too. It seemed much more natural and truly representative of the way I was feeling than taking the role that I had always 'acted' before. I learned a lesson from this incident. That it is better to express sadness when sadness is being felt. The family members most assuredly thought no less of me or my abilities for this human expression. They knew it was how I truly felt and that I was grieving with them."

How comforting Dr. Hicks's love and heartfelt concern must have been for that hurting family. (I know, because he's held my hand many times, too.) He isn't afraid to show his patients that he's not only caring for them professionally but also that he cares about them with his heart. Once they understand that, they are able to respond much more readily to the encouragement he gives them. For example, he repeatedly tells those who are in mourning because of losing an eye that "one eye is a necessity, but two are a luxury." When he counsels patients who are diagnosed with macular degeneration, a condition in which the central visual field is lost, he points out that the disease will probably not rob them of their "side" vision, their peripheral sight. He convinces them that while no magical escape exists from such insurmountable problems, as someone once said, they can learn to live with mountains that will not move.

The patients who are best equipped to face whatever "mountains" appear in their path, said Dr. Hicks, "are those fortunate men and women who have an enduring faith in God" and who understand that health problems occur in this imperfect world "by gene transmission, by environment, or by accident.

They know that God is on his throne and that he listens to their prayers. They also know that miracles still do happen."

"Gracious God, thank you for the gift of sight. Help me use it to see the joyful blessings you have given me and to see ways to bring that joy to others. Amen."

COMPANIONS YOU CAN COUNT ON

Sheila Walsh

God sets the lonely in families, he leads forth the prisoners with singing; but the rebellious live in a sun-scorched land.

PSALM 68:6

Sometimes, when I can't sleep, I lie in bed, and instead of counting sheep, I count all the fun people God has put in my life. On one such occasion, I'd gone to bed at 10:30 and quickly fallen asleep. When I woke up, I was sure it must be morning and was shocked to see that the clock on my bedside table said it was only 12:30. I looked at my husband, and he was out cold.

I slipped out of bed and checked on the baby. Christian had crawled to the far end of his crib and was dreamily sucking his thumb and holding his favorite blue blanket against his cheek.

I went downstairs, made some hot tea, and switched on the television to my favorite channel, Nickelodeon. I watched *I Love Lucy* and Dick Van Dyke, but I was still wide awake. When the clock said it was 3:30, I went back upstairs determined to fall asleep.

That's when I started to imagine Luci, Patsy, Marilyn, Barbara, and Thelma jumping over a fence. Then I remembered some of the stories they tell when they speak at the conferences, and I started to laugh. I don't know if you've ever felt like laughing while the person next to you is fast asleep, but it makes you laugh more. I stuck my head under the covers to try to muffle my snorts.

I couldn't help myself. I was recalling Luci's story about the Chihuahua in which Luci, as the loser of a bet with Marilyn, had to go up to a stranger and tell her that her Chihuahua was so much better and to thank her for her prayers. Then there's Luci's story about the time she put the name Bernadette Apes down on the visitor's card in a small neighborhood church, not realizing that the pastor would call out her name from the pulpit and attempt to engage her in conversation.

Now, as I lay in bed at 3:30 A.M., I'm almost choking under the bed covers. Barry sleeps on.

These wonderful women I travel with on The Joyful Journey have brought so much joy and friendship to me. Their presence in my life is all the more bounteous a gift when I remember how I used to find it hard to make deep friendships with other women. I felt such a need for approval and acceptance; yet I was afraid to let the real me be seen in case I wasn't enough—and I was pretty sure I wasn't. The higher I erected a façade of fear around myself, the more I needed approval but the less I was available to receive it. Hiding behind that wall, I didn't realize how much effort it would take for someone to scale those heights to find the real, scared, and unsure me.

Finally, I figured out I was inadequate to create or maintain relationships. I never have been able to, and I never will. Fortunately, at the same time, I realized Christ is enough for all of us. His mercy helps us to see others mercifully, and his loving acceptance of us enables us to accept ourselves and others. With that as a beginning point, we can relax, be ourselves, and come out from behind the protective walls we've erected. Then we can connect with others who have discovered the joy of just being themselves—flawed and silly but of worth because of Jesus.

Who do you want to travel down life's highway with? Who can make you giggle and snort under the covers just thinking about them and their antics? What do you need to do to make yourself available for a deeper and richer relationship with them?

The next time you can't sleep, thank God for all those who make your life richer. And laugh a little as you watch them try to clear the fence!

"Lord,
Thank you for friends.
Thank you for family.
Thank you that we are part of your family forever.
Amen."

EATING WITH GLADNESS

Marilyn Meberg

Go, eat your food with gladness, and drink your wine with a joyful heart, for it is now that God favors what you do.

ECCLESIASTES 9:7

Well, finally, one of life's major quandaries has been settled: Frozen turkeys are more flavorful than unfrozen or free-range. For years I have harbored the suspicion that I ought never to buy a frozen turkey if I wanted a truly memorable and tasty turkey dinner. I ought, instead, to choose a fresh, free-range turkey that had lightheartedly poked about the farm without restriction. It only seemed logical that this happy, carefree life would produce a flavorful turkey.

However, this logic was never supported by actual experience. For years, each of our carefully selected free-range turkeys was a bit dry, and the flavor never lived up to our expectations. I figured each year we unwittingly chose a turkey who was a malcontent and simply did not have the motivation or imagination to thrive in its free-range status. That being the case, it might as well have climbed a perch and stayed there until its number was called.

My newfound knowledge about the superiority of frozen turkeys came as a result of findings by the consumer reporter on *Good Morning America.* With the cooperation of one of the finest cooking schools in New York City, four of the top cooking students were asked to choose which of three roasted turkeys was the most flavorful: the frozen, unfrozen, or free-range. With no background knowledge of the three turkeys, each student chef chose the previously frozen turkey as the most flavorful.

Then the TV staff was put to the same test, and they, too, chose the once-frozen turkey.

Well, that settled it for me! Since Thanksgiving was only a few days away, I snapped off the TV and hurried off to buy a frozen turkey. I stood in front of three enclosed cases and stared at their contents. A number of brand-name turkeys were lying in there, but I wasn't familiar with any of the names. I assumed that I should just find the weight I wanted and be off with him or her.

To see the written poundage on each label, I practically had to crawl inside the case and rummage around what felt like a pile of cold boulders. With each movement of the turkeys, I unsettled their configuration. They started to rumble dangerously about. I quickly grabbed a sixteen-pound Jenny O and slammed shut the case, averting a massive avalanche of cascading Jennies heading for the floor.

The directions on Jenny's frozen back instructed me to place her in my refrigerator where she would thaw herself to perfection. I would take it from there on Thanksgiving Day.

With innocent anticipation, I pulled Jenny out of the refrigerator Thanksgiving morning to prepare her for the trip to my oven. She wasn't as stiff as the day we had met, but she certainly wasn't soft and pliable. Soaking her in cold water in the kitchen sink and instructing her to hurry up and thaw, I made a fabulous breakfast of Belgian waffles, bacon, and fruit compote, which would hopefully satisfy the family hunger for more hours than I had originally thought.

Jenny crawled into my oven around eleven o'clock and came out around five in the evening. She was flavorful and moist until I cut more than an inch deep. Then we hit pink meat, which threw me into fits about salmonella potential. We sliced surface pieces all around the body, and later I placed Jenny in a huge stewing pot to cook more thoroughly for future soups and casseroles. (Forget about sandwiches the next day!)

In spite of this mild turkey crisis, my family, some dear friends, and I had a wonderful time together. We laughed, caught up with the events in our respective lives, and even reminisced about the time our golden retriever almost succeeded in pulling a perfectly cooked Thanksgiving turkey off the unattended serving platter. His intention apparently was to sneak out the back door for a private meal.

Coming back to the present and looking into the faces of my kids and friends, I remembered something I knew but often forgot. What makes a gathering meaningful is family and friends. The ingredients for sweet fellowship rest not upon frozen or free-range turkeys but upon a mutuality of love and caring.

Sometimes I forget and allow myself to focus on the externals of a celebration, which, of course, throttles my internal experience of joy. Even if we had been reduced to ordering out for pizza and having Jenny join us in eating the meal, we would have had a great time simply because we were together.

Now, that doesn't mean I won't enter into the turkey debate again; however, I've pretty much decided next Thanksgiving I'll go back to cooking the malcontents from the free-range farm. At least they're nearly ready for the oven when they come in the door.

"Lord, thank you for the blessing of family and friends and loving relatedness. Thank you that your presence in our lives is constant and your love for us unwavering. Thank you for the small giggles about turkeys and that you bid us to eat with a joyful heart simply because you favor us as members of your divine family. Amen."

UNCLE BROTHER

Thelma Wells

I will turn their mourning into gladness;
I will give them comfort and joy instead of sorrow.

JEREMIAH 31:13

One of the most colorful people in my family is Uncle Lawrence Morris, Jr., my mother's only brother. His nickname is Uncle Brother. At more than seventy years old, he tries to act and think like a springtime chicken. He's always talking about his girlfriend, but I don't think he really has one. At least no one in the family has seen any sign of her!

Sixteen years ago, I became Uncle Brother's legal guardian because he was termed a "chronic alcoholic." Although he had accepted Christ as a young man, Uncle Brother had lived like the devil. He admits he has had his share of booze and all that goes with it. When he reached the point all he wanted was his drinking, someone had to care for him, and that someone turned out to be me. As his guardian, I made decisions he didn't agree with, but we couldn't deal with each other on level ground as one adult to another. It was a dark night in our relationship, and we didn't know if the morning would ever dawn.

But even when I was angry with him for the way he treated everyone, I prayed for him to return to the Lord. I prayed for the Holy Spirit to convict him and to give him no rest until he repented and started to live for God. I didn't want Uncle Brother to die without realizing he could enjoy a better life than the one he had chosen. He knew I loved him because I put up with him. And I often told him I loved him in spite of the way he responded to me when I said it.

Thanks be to God, we made it through that night; our sorrow turned to joy. For the past several years, Uncle Brother has made some major changes. Now he talks about how God has brought him through dangers seen and unseen. He praises God in song. He watches Christian television. He reads his Bible. He bridles his tongue. He speaks affectionately about people. He has changed his friends. He is respected in his community. He is concerned about other family members. He attends family celebrations. He's fun to be around. His mourning has turned to gladness and so has everyone else's in the family.

With my uncle, weeping endured for about ten years, but God was always present. He never left Uncle Brother alone. And he was waiting for my uncle to reopen his heart.

We endured turbulence and turmoil as the norm for years. But today, my uncle can sing with me, "This joy we have, the world didn't give it and the world can't take it away!"

Are you dealing with someone whom you feel will never change? Do you vacillate between wishing he would change and just wanting him to leave you alone? Have you given up expecting good things from that person?

Nobody is so far from God that he can't get back to the Lord. Our responsibility is to keep knocking at God's door about that person, to keep believing God will answer our prayers. Thank God for what he will do. Patiently but expectantly wait on the Lord. Renew your hope!

"Lord, that you never give up on us is more consoling than I can express. Just to watch you move people from the pits of hell to the portholes of glory is overwhelming. Let me always remember that because you made us you can change us. Increase my patience with those who seem like hopeless causes. And renew my persistence in praying for them. Amen."

SURPRISE PACKAGE

Barbara Johnson

The LORD is my strength and my shield; my heart trusts in him, and I am helped. My heart leaps for joy and I will give thanks to him in song.

PSALM 28:7

The publisher of several of my books held a contest among bookstore owners to see who could come up with the cleverest way to display my "stuff"—books, joy boxes, coffee mugs, calendars, and other items. No one told me until the contest was over that I was the prize! But, as things turned out, I was the one who ended up feeling like the winner.

When the top display was named at the New Orleans Baptist Book Store, Bill and I flew there to host a book-signing and to meet all the employees. Then I was invited to speak at the Baptist seminary and also at a marriage seminar. During the few hours we had free during that trip, I had arranged to drive one hundred miles to McComb, Mississippi, to have lunch with a Spatula friend and her daughter.

I was anticipating being with these gals as a quiet interlude in the busy schedule the publisher had set up for me, but when we arrived, the "little lunch" for the four of us had turned into a meeting with more than four hundred women at the local Ramada Inn! My friend never was very good at keeping secrets. When I expressed shock at having four hundred women instead of just us four, she shrugged and smiled apologetically.

"Word just got around somehow," she said, adding that the last "celebrity" who had come to their town was Barry Goldwater—and that was twenty years ago!

My friend had arranged for the local Christian bookstore to load up with stacks of books to sell (and for me to sign), and long lines of women soon formed wanting to buy books or to get a bear hug from Bill.

As I looked at my watch, I remembered that little quip that says schedules are like piñatas: They're made to be broken. The place was packed, with all those women crowded into an area designed to hold 350. There wasn't enough room. There wasn't enough food. There wasn't enough silverware. And when I looked at the crowd, I wasn't sure I had enough energy to give them what they expected.

But from the moment we had driven through the jam-packed parking lot and stopped at the front door of the hotel, I had sensed something was special about this group. As I walked in the door, I heard laughter—one of my favorite sounds!

It was such a joy to be with those exuberant women. I shared my story with them, and in return they blessed me with their laughter, their care, and their love. It was an unexpected pleasure that became the highlight of my whole trip. I felt as if I had won a prize!

Whenever I find myself feeling weary and overwhelmed by the commitments I've made to my family, friends, publishers, and the Joyful Journey tour, I remember that day in McComb, Mississippi, and remember Jesus' words: "From everyone who has been given much, much will be demanded; and from the one who has been entrusted with much, much more will be asked" (Luke 12:48).

Bill and I were shocked to see the abundance of women there to greet us, but we were energized by their contagious enthusiasm. Our little visit had turned into a big surprise that exhausted us—but also thrilled us.

Many blessings have been given to me: More joy than I ever imagined having, more love than I ever dreamed I'd know, more encouragement than I deserve. But I know God didn't bless me with these gifts so I could sit back in the recliner and keep them all to myself.

Sometimes life becomes so complicated we feel as if we've gone as far as we can down this stressful highway. We imagine ourselves smashed up against a brick wall, unable to answer one more call, hear one more complaint, and take one more breath. When that's the image that fills your mind, change the brick wall to God. Imagine yourself pressed tightly against his heart, wrapped in his everlasting arms, soothed by his life-giving breath. Picture yourself encircled in God's love, soaked in his strength. Then step out onto the highway once more.

"Dear God, I press myself against your heart and ask that you hold me in your arms, shield me with your mighty angels, and empower me with your love. Amen."

KOOKY COWORKERS

Thelma Wells

As God's fellow workers we urge you not to receive God's grace in vain.

2 CORINTHIANS 6:1

Picture this: You are asked to travel for most of the weekends of an entire year around the country with five women you've never met. You'll be speaking together, eating together, and praying together. You'll be under pressure together, and you'll share in the joys and tribulations of traveling together. That's an awful lot of togetherness with a bunch of strangers, if you ask me.

Well, if I had known what it was going to be like to travel the country with these five Women of Faith coworkers, I would have . . . why, I would have clambered to sign up for the adventure a lot sooner. I had no idea how exciting and vibrant they were, nor what an influence they would have on my life.

Here's an insider's view of my five kooky coworkers:

I will always remember the time Barbara Johnson presented me with a silly pair of bumblebee house slippers in front of sixteen thousand women in Pittsburgh. Those bright yellow and black slippers were adorned with big, white, flannel wings, as if they were ready to take off flying over the audience and were going to take me with them. All day long at the conference, throngs of ladies came by to view my feet adorned in those silly slippers. They brought a lot of attention to the message that you can be the best of what you want to BEE in Christ. If anyone exemplifies that message, it's Barbara, who has overcome so much sorrow to spread so much joy.

Marilyn Meberg has the kookiest way of making me laugh. She can just start smiling and crescendo into a powerful laugh—about absolutely nothing. She starts with ha—ha, ha—ha, ha, ha—ha, ha, ha, ha—and bursts into contagious guffawing. Before you know you it, everybody, including me, is falling over laughing and not knowing why—except you know you're laughing with (or is it at?) Marilyn. What joy to laugh for the sake of laughing. I'm plumb worn out from all this hilarity over nothin' and wouldn't give it up for a sober moment for anything.

I love to hear Patsy Clairmont say, "I don't think so!" With her hands on her hips, her knees bent, her chin up, and her head in the air, Patsy's posture proclaims that life is ridiculous, and she knows it. When she says, "I don't think so," you better listen up and learn. She's a little woman with great perception. When Patsy speaks, Thelma listens.

Sheila Walsh is uninhibited. One day when we were filming a video for the Women of Faith conferences, as she stood in front of the camera, without warning, she broke away from the script and interjected several lines that were so funny everybody in the room whooped. We laughed so hard we struggled to get back to being serious. But then again, we were being too serious anyway. We women were seriously trying to remember our lines. The camera people were seriously filming it all. And the producer was serious about everything. Leave it to Sheila to splash some uninhibited humor into our situation.

Sometimes, as we other speakers rise to give our talks, Sheila likes to encourage us by putting her fingers in her mouth and whistling. Afterwards, she innocently looks around, as if to say, "What's wrong with the whistle? Doesn't everybody respond like that?" Sure, Sheila, all the time.

The very first gift I received from these women was given to me by Luci Swindoll. Luci walked up to me with her hand behind her back and said she wanted to give me something she had recently seen in a store. She pulled out a bumblebee finger

puppet on her index finger and suggested I wear it that night at the Women of Faith Conference. I did, and we all had a good laugh over it—what else? That's Luci: creative, playful, and always up for providing a reason to laugh.

Through all the pain, sorrow, disappointment, aggravation, and agitation of life, these wonderful women are still funny, adventurous, and silly.

Just as they have influenced and encouraged me, broadened my horizons, and made me laugh, you, too, can be a blessing to the people you meet today. Yes, life has its serious moments. But being just a bit kooky may be the secret to seeing yourself and others through good times and bad. Go ahead, make someone's day—make her smile.

"Master, you have given us the ability to laugh as well as cry, to be silly as well as serious, to be kooky people. Thank you for putting people in our lives who remind us that the quality of life is what we make it. Help us to be more aware of the ways we can encourage others and ignite the fires of joy in their lives. Thank you for how you lighten our heavy loads and give us words of cheer in our spirits every day when we listen to you. Amen."

LITTLE REMINDERS

Barbara Johnson

Let your light shine before men, that they may see your good deeds and praise your Father in heaven.

MATTHEW 5:16

Unable to find what I needed in a store recently, I sought out a salesperson for assistance. Finally I found one of the red-vested clerks, but he was bent over a large box, focused on a search of his own.

Seeing his resolute face and hurried manner, I hesitated to interrupt him. Then I spotted the nametag bouncing around on the shoulder of his vest. It bore a smiley face.

And below his name, Caleb, was this statement: "Ask me! I like to help."

Encouraged by that suggestion, I cleared my throat and said, "Excuse me, please. Could you help me?"

Caleb jerked his head out of the box and then straightened up when he saw me. Suddenly his seriousness was transformed into a warm smile. "Yes, ma'am! What can I do for you?" That smiley face and the message on Caleb's nametag had reassured me that I could expect a kind response from him. The incident reminded me of the messages and symbols we Christians wear to tell others who we are. (It's also a little like we senior citizens who wear nametags to our fiftieth high school reunions—to remind ourselves who we are!) How reassuring it is to see one of those little symbols when we need to approach a stranger to ask for help or to make some other request.

My son Barney knows all about that. A few years ago, when he owned a concrete business, a mishap occurred on one of his residential jobs. He was pouring concrete around someone's swimming pool when one of the side panels of the form collapsed and some of the concrete oozed onto a neighbor's property. By the time he got the mixer turned off and the chute closed up, there was an awful calamity!

He dreaded telling the neighbor what had happened. He imagined the person ranting, raving, and threatening lawsuits and all sorts of grievances when he or she saw the problem Barney's accident had created. So when Barney walked up the neighbor's driveway, his heart was pounding and his palms were sweating.

Then, as he walked by the neighbor's car, he saw something that eased his worries. There, just above the back bumper, was a simple decal—two curved lines that started at a point and ended by crossing over each other. A little fish.

Encouraged by that wordless promise, Barney rang the doorbell. When the woman answered the door, he showed her the problem, apologized for the mess, and promised to restore everything fully and pay for any other damages the escaping concrete might have caused. The woman listened in silence to all that Barney had to say. Then he ended up with, "I was really apprehensive about coming and telling you this, but then I saw the little fish on your car, and I thought, *Thank you, Lord! She's a Christian! She'll understand—and she'll forgive me.*"

And sure enough, the woman did. (After all, what else could she do once Barney had pointed out the symbol she'd stuck on her car for all to see?) She graciously accepted Barney's apology and even invited him inside for a glass of ice water. It takes courage to wear the symbols of Christianity. As soon as you slap a fish-shaped decal on your car, some turkey shows up at your door, saying he's just dumped a load of concrete all over your patio. While you're reading that Christian magazine in the checkout line, the two-year-old behind you is swiping your white, wool skirt with a dripping chocolate ice cream cone.

As soon as you pin that little cross to your lapel, one of your kids walks in the door and asks you to tell a little white lie—just this once—to get him out of big trouble at school.

It's much easier to wear a Christian symbol under your coat or carry it in your purse—or hide it under a bushel. It takes real courage to hang it out there for all the world to see. Whether you wear a tiny, fish-shaped lapel pin or paint "Truckin' for Jesus" in letters two feet high on the side of your eighteen-wheeler, it's all the same to those who are watching. For some of them, the only Jesus they've ever known is the Jesus they see in you.

"Gracious Father, please fill me with your light so my short-comings are overshadowed and your goodness shines through. Amen."

ENJOY THE VIEW

Sheila Walsh

May your father and mother be glad; may she who gave you birth rejoice!

PROVERBS 23:25

I had no idea it would be this wonderful! Sure, I had watched my sister as she cared for her sons and saw her joy at every little step they took. But I had no idea having my own child would be like landing over the rainbow and waking up in Oz.

I also had no idea my body could be stretched to those proportions without bursting or that my heart could either. I've noticed too that in the few moments of sleep you get when your children are babies, God mysteriously and wondrously tucks love into your heart. You find your ocean of love is so deep it can carry you across the rough water of sleeplessness. Billy Sunday said, "Mothers ... fill places so great that there isn't an angel in heaven who wouldn't be glad to give a bushel of diamonds to come down here and take their place."

But it's just for a moment. That's how it seems to me already as I watch Christian sit up and crawl. There's a whole world of growing and being and going ahead of him, and if Barry and I do a good job, Christian will be a strong, independent man. One day I'll watch him look into the eyes of a young woman in a white dress, and his eyes will be full of her.

But for tonight I get to tuck him into bed. I'll enjoy the scenery of his face, and I'll watch as his little lips move in his sleep. I'll enjoy how his hair curls at the bottom of his neck and tucks into his pajamas. And I'll sing to him a song of celebration I wrote when he was born.

"Lay your tiny golden head upon this pillow, dear.
There are angels watching over you
And the morning star is in the heavens close to you.
Can you see the moon is shining in your room
Tying silver ribbons in your hair?
May your sleep be sweet until the sun brings morning here.
And I never knew such a tender love
That could break my heart in two.
So I lay down gently now at Jesus' feet with you.
And I feel I'm lying on holy ground,
Such a gift God gave us in you.
So I kiss your velvet cheek and say a prayer for you.
Lay your tiny, golden head upon this pillow, dear.
There are angels watching over you.
And the morning star is in the heavens close to you."

Perhaps your children are all grown or you have no children. But look around you and see what you have. It may be a tail-waggin' dog who welcomes you home. Or a husband who notices you don't feel well and runs you a hot bath. Or a friend who calls at just the right moment. Whatever you see, stop for a moment and enjoy the view.

"Lord Jesus,
Thank you for my life.
Thank you for those who make my life richer, warmer, funnier, stronger.
Help me to stop and enjoy the scenery today.
Amen."

L-L-L

Patsy Clairmont

And how delightful is a timely word!

PROVERBS 15:23 NASB

What kind of a communicator are you? Are you a babbling brook, a quiet stream, or a thunderous waterfall? Do you have volumes of verbiage like the *Encyclopædia Britannica?* Or are you a selective and simple speaker like a Dick and Jane primer? Most folks probably fall somewhere in between.

I'm more a whirlwind of words; I know that surprises you. Don't you wonder how a five-foot woman could have a ten-foot capacity for verbosity? Just lucky, I guess. Although some may take issue ... like my friend Lana.

Lana and I have been cohorts for years. We have had miles of smiles. We have traveled together, spoken at conferences together, spent holidays together, and played endless games of Scrabble. We laugh, squabble, commiserate, dream, debate, and converse.

Boy, can we converse! Well, okay, maybe I do tend to have a few more words to express than she does, but then, who's counting? Surely not me. I don't do numbers, just words. Actually, Lana can hold her own once she gets started. But my bursts of babble have been known to wear her down and out before she can begin.

I remember ... Lana and I had just completed an exciting but exhausting seminar. We were sharing a room, and I was wound tighter than a tick from days of working with fascinating people. My way to debrief was to release my thoughts in squalls, blustery reports of days of details. I'm usually aware when

I'm, say, too much for my listeners, but evidently this time I lost track of my mouth-monitor.

It wasn't that I had bored Lana into a mild stupor. No, evidently I had knocked her plumb out. I realized this when I hovered over her reclining frame to emphasize some critical point in my narrative. She was no longer conscious. Z's slipped effortlessly through her exhausted lips, and her eyelids were sealed like Ziploc baggies, suggesting our talk had been terminated. How rude! And I was just getting to the good part.

Since then Lana and I have chortled over that abbreviated conversation many times. She claims she had heard enough. I, on the other hand, know I had more to say . . . much, much more.

While some folks may need to cut back on fat grams, shopping sprees, and (or) television viewing (okay, I do too), a slew of us need to reduce our rambling recitals. Silence is not empty but, in fact, often fuller than our many words. So instead of trying to fill every quiet moment with chatter, we would do well to sit ever so still (shh) and develop a new skill: listening. In doing so we might hear the Z's of a companion attempting to get a well-deserved break. Or perhaps we would hear the Lord speaking ever so softly to us.

"Lord, please speak loud enough for us to hear you over our clamoring hearts. For some of us, even when we're not talking, we still have a lot of noise going on inside. We are amazed, Lord, that you never tire of hearing us talk to you. That's quite an extravagant truth—for no one has ever cared for us like that till you. Amen."

WIDE LOAD (I BEG YOUR PARDON!)

Stuff We Get to, Want to, Have to Lug Through Life

JUMPING THE GUN

Thelma Wells

Yet not my will, but yours be done.

LUKE 22:42

Have you ever watched runners during the Olympics preparing to start a race? They carefully position themselves in the starting blocks, placing their feet just so, and their hands on the ground in the way they have practiced for hours. Then, at the pop of the gun, they take off with everything in them.

But if one of the racers, too eager to get those mini-seconds of a head start, jumps out of the blocks before the gun sounds, a false start is declared, and everyone has to go through getting set in the blocks again. Sometimes a race can have two or three false starts. Everyone gets really tired, antsy, and irritable.

I've had a few false starts myself. At times I was so ready to rush out to grab God's will that I thought I heard the gun only to learn I'd jumped out of the blocks too soon. I remember one day writing down plans for a ministry building, furnishing it (in my mind), imagining the open house, and seeing the finished project before it began. I was set to leap out of those starting blocks.

Then a chance to purchase a building came up. And I was off! I believed God was saying, "This is it, kid." I believed I even heard God's voice (in my spirit) telling me to purchase things, as if I owned that building. I bought the curtains, cooking utensils, dishes, floral arrangements, and candles for this new place. I knew he meant *now*.

But my plans for that building never worked out. I sought every avenue to purchase it but experienced only drawbacks, setbacks, and obstacles—lots of false starts. But, I'm the obstacle-jumpin' lady. I've even written a book about it, I'm such an authority on the subject.

Finally, I became impatient and a little angry because of the obstacles. Then I had enough sense to ask God what was going on. I asked him to take the desire for this building out of my mind if this wasn't his will for me. Almost instantly, the desire for the building left. Ain't that somethin'? I was agonizing over a plan that wasn't in God's timing or will for me. I was acting on my own desires. Thank God he kept calling out, "False start!"

When I didn't get the building I thought I was supposed to have, I waited until December 1997 for God to grant me what he had promised me—four years before. Here's how it happened. The landlord for the structure I had been occupying told me he was going to increase the cost of the lease by more than fifty percent.

So several days after his announcement, I started to drive around looking for lease or rent signs. During my drive, the Holy Spirit asked me, "Why are you wasting time? I already have a building for you." I stopped looking, turned around, and went grocery shopping.

The following evening, I was talking to family members about my problem. One of them said, "You know, that house on Cedar Crest is still vacant." I contacted the proper people, and within three weeks, my office was relocated in a beautiful facility that God had prepared for us before the idea of a ministry building ever entered my mind. When the time was right, we were off and running.

Two impatient people in the Bible knew all about jumping the gun and the consequences that can bring. Remember Sister Sarah and Brother Abraham? God told the two of them they would have a child. But waiting for nearly a century got on

Sarah's nerves. So she told Abraham to sleep with her handmaiden, Hagar.

Abraham didn't mention anything to Sarah about that being a false start. In fact, he didn't seem to have a problem with the idea at all. Hagar conceived a son, who by the customs of that day, became Sara's property. But this wasn't a happy ending. Hagar, the natural mother, ridiculed Sara because she couldn't have children.

Sarah grew irate and blamed Abraham for the trouble. She said, "You're responsible for the wrong I'm suffering."

Abraham, who was impatient himself, replied, "Do with her whatever you think best."

So Sarah mistreated Hagar, and Hagar ran away into the desert.

Now, God had told Abraham he would be the father of many nations. God's plan was to bless Sarah with a son. But Sarah was ninety and Abraham a hundred years old before their son, Isaac, was born. I admit, I probably would have gotten frustrated, too. But a whole lot of suffering could have been alleviated if Sarah and Abraham hadn't jumped the gun, rushing on ahead of God.

Have you ever had a dream or a creative idea that you believed came from God? Since it came from God, he must be telling you to do it now, right? In your mind you're thinking, *Oh, what a good God! He expects me to use my intellect, academic competence, position, status, accomplishments to take control of this situation and get what I'm after. I'm a logical, analytical human being. I know what I'll do, I'll just . . .*

When we surrender our will to the Father, as Jesus did, we don't need to be concerned about how things will come out. God has promised the very best for us. Waiting is hard, I know. But false starts don't get us anywhere we want to go, either.

"Father, as I try to do your will, I often jump the gun. Thank you for your patience toward me and your protection. I really don't mean any harm. When I start to edge off the racing block, keep me from moving out. Amen."

ALIVE AGAIN

Luci Swindoll

Every good and perfect gift is from above,
coming down from the Father of the heavenly lights,
who does not change like shifting shadows.

JAMES 1:17

"This joy that I have, the world didn't give it to me,
This joy that I have, the world didn't give it to me.
The world didn't give it . . .
And the world can't take it away."

Oh, my sisters, listen up! I've been singing that song for days, as I'm running around the house, in the street, at the grocery store, in restaurants. Everywhere. "This Joy That I Have" has become my song. Actually, Thelma gave me the song, but God gave me the joy.

Here's what happened: For fifteen years I've had sleep apnea, which is a disorder that causes one to hold one's breath during the night for long periods of time. More often than not, the person awakens repeatedly in an effort to breathe. Very little sleep results. There is never REM sleep, the deepest and most necessary of all.

Recently, in an overnight stay at a sleep clinic, I learned that in 102 minutes of so-called "sleep," I awakened myself 123 times, with 87 of those being apnea episodes, where I gasped for breath. I'm surprised I didn't die somewhere along the way.

But, instead of dying, I slept during most of my "waking" hours. I slept while talking on the phone or face-to-face. I slept while writing, reading, driving. I slept at the computer, standing in line, or sitting in a chair. I slept at meetings, while eating, in moving vehicles, or while they were parked. I fell asleep midsentence. I slept at parties or in the quietness of my own home, at my desk, or standing at the stove. I slept all the time, and I drove my loved ones to distraction.

They begged me to get help, but I put it off. I kept thinking I would get better, the condition would go away, or Jesus would come.

Now we know I never really slept, night or day. I just dozed. I even dozed on the Joyful Journey platform. My greatest fear was I'd fall asleep during my own message. I didn't, and we all considered it a miracle.

Then I got brave. I phoned a specialist and found the cure. It's called a CPAP unit. It's a heaven-sent contraption that fits like a mask over my nose, permitting me to breathe deeply for the first time in almost two decades. I actually sleep! The air comes only through the nose so there's no sound from the mouth. I can't yawn, talk, snore, or draw in air with the mask. I can do only one thing . . . sleep. It's wonderful.

So what if I'm funny looking? So what if I sleep with a tube of air attached? So what if I just increased my carry-on luggage by another bag? I don't care because I'm sleeping, girls. It's fabulous!

If you've put off something you know needs attention, put it off no longer. Get up now and make the phone call that will change your life. Reach out and take the gift God wants to give you. Stop procrastinating. His gifts are good and perfect.

I'm a new woman. I'm alive again, singing, dancing, and bouncing off the ceiling. I'm wearing my friends out. Oh, well, I may have to get a new set of friends, anyway. Ones with more energy.

"This joy that I have, the world . . ."

"Father, thank you that your gifts are good and perfect. Thank you for your provision for us. Prompt us to be responsible and attentive when we need to do something, and help us do it now. Amen."

ANXIETY OVER THE UNSEEN

Marilyn Meberg

Do not be anxious about anything.

PHILIPPIANS 4:6

Here, lady, I got a fork and spoon for ya." I looked into the grubby little face of a five- or six-year-old boy whom I had been eyeballing uneasily before I ever took my place in the cafeteria line. He had been standing guard over the utensils while his oblivious mother piled her plate with macaroni and cheese. He, in turn, handed out silverware to whoever would take it from him. The gesture in itself was innocent enough and actually rather sweet. What troubled me was his fingering each utensil not by the handle but by the part that would ultimately be in my mouth. I have a bit of a "germ-thing," so I was torn between not wanting to hurt his feelings and not wanting to encounter whatever germ culture was represented on his dirty little hands.

As I approached him, I was struck by a flash of brilliance. I bent down and in a confidential whisper told him I didn't need any silver because I always ate with my hands.

His eyes brightened with envy as he said, "You do? Does your mom let you do that, really?"

Jerking my head in Luci's direction, I said, "She doesn't see very well, and usually she can't make out what I'm doing anyway."

He looked over at Luci and then back at me. "Wow, what a great mom!"

As I made my way around the entrée counter, I rehearsed in my mind yet again why I didn't like cafeterias. Even if no well-intentioned but dirty little utensil boy were there, other hygienically questionable people were. And they all touched the serving spoon handles. I noted people often sloshed a bit of sauce on their hands, licked them clean, and then, with their newly slicked fingers, reached for the next serving spoon. How did I know they didn't have trench mouth germs, which would then take up residence on the spoon handle waiting for me?

Okay, maybe these people didn't have trench mouth, but maybe they had an incontinent parakeet whose cage they had tidied up just prior to coming to the cafeteria. Or what about the guy wearing the "Digby O'Dell Mortuary" shirt who was sifting through the fried chicken container in search of drumsticks? Was it just my imagination that those drumsticks seemed to stiffen at his touch?

"How long have you had this germ thing?" Luci asked after questioning why I was eating my entire meal with an oversized spoon I had found in an obscure container hidden slightly behind the soft ice-cream machine.

"Since the sixth grade."

"What happened in the sixth grade?"

"Our science teacher had us all touch some specially treated sponge, and overnight it grew bacteria cultures that we watched develop into various colorful and horrifying configurations. I've never been the same since."

Luci slowly put down her fork and studied it for a second. Then, with renewed enthusiasm, she announced, "If those germs haven't gotten me by this time in my life, I don't think they ever will!"

Her healthy response reminded me that for me to fear the unseen and worry about its potential to do harm throttles my joy. Of course one should observe hygienic health practices, but if carried to an extreme, they can lead to wrestling with a too-large spoon in a cafeteria with plenty of right-sized forks. Not only that, but also God has created within each of us a miraculously

effective immune system designed to ward off the consequences of grubby fingers.

Fortified by those encouraging thoughts, I headed back to the utensil containers for a fork. Of course, I must admit this brave action was encouraged by noting that the little grunge-fellow hadn't been near the utensil counter for at least ten minutes. . . . He was finishing his mother's macaroni.

"Lord, so many experiences in life make us anxious and steal our joy. Help us to keep everything in perspective and to rest in your provision. Thank you for your patience and love during those times when our thinking gets out of whack. Thank you that you bring us back to that centered place where we can be 'anxious about nothing.' Amen."

I COULD BE A GREAT CHRISTIAN IF . . .

Sheila Walsh

I do not understand what I do. For what I want to do I do not do, but what I hate I do.

ROMANS 7:15

I could be so godly, if people didn't get in my face! It's dealing with all these humans that's doing me in.

This struggle came home powerfully to me when Barry, Christian, and I flew into Tulsa for a Women of Faith conference. We wanted to arrive Thursday afternoon or early evening, but the best flight time we could arrange put us into Tulsa after 10 P.M. Christian had been good during the trip, but we could tell, as we waited for our luggage at the airport, that he was very tired.

We had been told the hotel would send a courtesy van to pick us up because we had so much stuff, especially baby paraphernalia. But we saw no sign of the van once our bags finally showed up. Barry called the hotel in case they had forgotten about the arrangement. I could tell by his body language that he was becoming angry.

I knelt down beside the baby in his stroller. "This is when daddies like mommies to stay out of the way!" I said. "So we had better wait over here."

After fifteen minutes Barry came over to us. He was very upset. "The guy at the front desk said they were too busy, and we should catch a cab. When I told him we had too much stuff for a taxi, and we also had a six-month-old baby, he said, 'That's really not my problem' and hung up."

"How rude!" I said. "Oh well, let's take two cabs." We bundled into two cabs, and when we arrived at the hotel, Barry went inside to talk to the manager on duty. Christian and I decided to wait outside. After a little while, Barry hadn't reappeared so we went in to see what was happening. He was standing at the front desk arguing with two of the hotel staff. I overheard one of the insults directed at Barry, and something in me snapped. I marched over to the desk and told the red-faced employee that he was a jerk. We got our key and finally made it to our room.

Once the baby was settled for the night, I ran a bath. As I lay in the soothing water, I started a litany of all the reasons it was so hard to be a Christian—and all of those reasons boiled down to having to relate to people. Just as I was working my way into sputtering to God about how offensive people can be, I realized I was rationalizing my own behavior. I became overwhelmed by what I had said to those two hotel clerks.

I thought, *I'm here with the Women of Faith conference. I'm here to talk about God's love, and I just called the guy at the front desk a jerk. How can I possibly walk on stage tomorrow night?* I felt like such a hypocrite.

So I did the only thing I knew to do: I threw myself on God's mercy and asked him what I should do now. His response was as clear as a sunny day after a rain. God didn't speak to me in an audible voice, but I knew he was telling me to get out of the bath, dress, go downstairs, and ask for forgiveness. I dried off, pulled on jeans and a shirt, and headed for the door.

"Where are you going?" Barry asked, apparently worried I was ready for round two with the desk clerk.

"It's okay, honey," I said. "I'll be right back."

I dragged myself along the corridor to the elevator. It was now after midnight, we hadn't eaten for a long time, and I'd taken off all my makeup. I looked like I'd been in a train wreck. The doors opened in the lobby, and I walked toward the front desk. The two men were standing there with arms folded, watching me as I approached.

"I've come down to ask you to forgive me," I said. "What I said to you was so wrong, and I'm sorry."

They looked at me as if I had just confessed to shooting John Lennon.

Finally, one of them said, "I'm sorry, too."

Well, that's all I needed to hear. I could have run up the fifteen flights of stairs (figuratively speaking, of course). I had headed down to the lobby with no joy and weighed down by my sin, but I returned to our room lighter than air because I was forgiven.

I don't tell you this story to suggest I'm proud of what happened. Far from it. I deeply regret when I dishonor God with my life, but I want you to know that none of us is alone in her struggles. When, like the apostle Paul, we do the thing we don't want to do, we are given an opportunity to put it right.

Are you having trouble living the Christian life because of people? Maybe, like me, you need to examine what responsibility you bear for the situation. What steps can you take to get right with God and to make amends to the people you have offended or hurt?

"Lord Jesus, I make so many mistakes. Thank you that you forgive me and wash me clean. Thank you for loving me. Tell me how to right any wrongs I've committed. Amen."

W-W-J-D? L-O-V-E!

Barbara Johnson

Love one another. As I have loved you,
so you must love one another.

John 13:34

An amazing phenomenon is sweeping the country. It's just a simple thing, and many would say it's not even new, but from coast to coast young people and oldies as well are adorning themselves with this latest fad, a bracelet which consists of nothing more than four little letters: WWJD.

Of course there's a secret behind the letters; they stand for a question, a simple but potent little idea that has the power to work extraordinary changes in all who understand what the four little letters mean. In the moment it takes the eye to focus and the brain to comprehend, the little letters can change anger into patience, apathy into concern, bigotry into tolerance, harshness into kindness. . . . The power is endless.

What do the letters mean? They ask the question, "What would Jesus do?" Wouldn't he reach out to the hurting, the lonely, the one caught up in sin and cast out by others? Wouldn't he offer kindness, patience, and love to those modern-day Samaritans who disagree with Christian values? If we apply those four little words to how we react to others, we find an answer that heals our relationships, promotes unity, and discourages difference. That small phrase can be the oil on troubled waters.

The power of this choice has worked its wonders in my life many times. The most memorable example occurred during an afternoon break one Saturday during the Joyful Journey tour, when all the speakers' book tables were swarmed by women hoping to buy a book, calendar, or other souvenir of the happy occasion. As I talked with the customers and happily sold books, I felt a tug on my sleeve. One of my friends who helps me at my table was bent over the stack of books, leaning forward, her head down but her face turned upward into the lowered faces of . . . good heavens, two men! Finding them there in the hustling, bustling sea of females swirling around the book table was like finding a bean in a box of oatmeal—quite a surprise.

Without letting her eyes drop from theirs, the helper had reached out to her left and grabbed my sleeve as she continued to listen to them. I sidled up to her and flashed the two young men my brightest smile. But the smiles they returned to me were tight and pained. My heart gave a lurch inside my chest. I had seen that look before.

"Let's talk," I told them. Somehow we managed to work our way out of the crowd like salmon swimming upstream; we finally found a quiet spot in a corner of the coliseum hallway. There, they quickly poured out their stories.

They were both homosexuals. And they were HIV positive; one already had AIDS. They had been raised in Christian homes, but now they were alienated from their families because they were gay. Working now as ushers at the Joyful Journey event, they had heard me talk about my own homosexual son and how I had learned through painful mistakes that the only thing I could do to help my son was to love him with the same love Jesus gave me. Long ago, I realized there is a division of labor: It's God's job to fix my kid; it's my job to love him.

"We've been to church, but the only thing we've heard there is that we're going to hell," one of them said sadly.

"Jesus loves you," I told them. "God loves you; you are his children. And I love you, too."

"No one ever told us that," one of the young men said quietly, his voice trembling.

Behind the young men, my escort was pointing toward the auditorium, tapping her watch, and mouthing the words, "We have to go!" I gathered the two of them into my arms, bent my head next to theirs, and offered a quick prayer. As I held them there, the pin of the little button I wear was pressing into my skin, reminding me of its message: "Someone Jesus Loves Has AIDS." What a privilege to have God use my arms to comfort these two sad, young men.

As I hurried to the auditorium, I wrote down their phone numbers (on my hand, my most common memo pad) and promised to call them. Later that night, we talked for nearly two hours. They asked me to phone their mothers, and I did. And my message to them was the same gentle question: WWJD?

The answer, I now know, is love.

"Dear Jesus, the answer is so simple. Please remind me always to ask the question and do what you would do. Amen."

MISSING IN ACTION

Patsy Clairmont

My people have been lost sheep.

JEREMIAH 50:6

Do you know what I'm tired of? Of course you don't, but I asked that so I could tell you. I have to tell someone because it's pressing down on my threadbare nerves. I'm tired of looking for things. There, I said it. I spend a great deal of energy—mental and physical—looking for lost, misplaced, and hidden stuff. I find the hunt frustrating, even maddening, and frequently unnecessary.

Take my glasses. You might as well; someone does every time I set them down. I often have to solicit my family's help in searching the premises for my bifocals. My family thinks I should hire my own posse because of the frequency with which I need help rounding up my belongings. I'm afraid they're right.

Keys, purse, and vital papers elude me. I know they can't walk off, but I have wondered if the Tidy Bowl Brother who constantly taps inside my clock has something to do with my ongoing dilemma. Maybe he has a trap door, and he and his brother rifle through my belongings and then scurry off to hide my stuff. All right, all right. I know it's my absentminded personality, not the Tidy Bowl Brother.

Here's what I think would help me and others prone to lostness—Velcro. More specifically, Velcro bodies. Think about it. Instead of laying down my glasses, I'd just press them on the outside of my upper arm. Then, when I needed them, I'd have them. The same with my keys. I could press my car key on one ear lobe and the house key on the other. Practical, handy, and within an arm's reach at any given moment.

Of course, the Velcro thing could get tricky when people shook hands or, worse yet, hugged. Getting shed of the other person might be touchy if not painful. And what if we Velcroed our glasses onto someone else without realizing it?

Oh, never mind. Back to the drawing board.

Velcro couldn't help me with my directions anyway. First off, I lose numbers. They just slip through my brain like money through my fingers. Second, I don't have a working grip on north, south, east, and west. And third, I'm a tad off-center, and when under pressure, I can't remember my right from my left. Now, on a calm day, that's not a problem. But when I'm searching for, say, a specific street and traffic is heavy, I've been known to turn into one-way traffic—all headed toward me!

Nothing is worse than not knowing where you are. I remember flying into an airport in southern California and waiting for someone to pick me up. No one came. To make matters worse, I didn't know the names of the people who were supposed to tend to me. After an extended wait, the Skycaps took note of my ongoing presence and became concerned. They even stopped anyone who drove slowly past the outdoor luggage retrieval and asked them if they were looking for me. How embarrassing.

It turned out my driver was at another airport waiting for me. The Skycaps were flipping coins to see who would adopt me when finally I was paged. My driver, relieved to find me, said she would be there as soon as she could. So, after another hour, when she pulled up, the Skycaps cheered her arrival. They ran my luggage to her car and wouldn't accept a tip. Their lost lamb had found her shepherdess.

Gratefully we do have a Shepherd—and he's not waiting at the wrong airport. He is the Good Shepherd who will seek out the stray lambs and bring them back to the safety of the fold. He promises he will never leave us or forsake us. He is one who sticks closer than a brother (or Velcro).

"Thank you, Lord, for understanding the extent of our lostness—and for never tiring of finding us. Amen."

HARMONY

Thelma Wells

Be joyful always; pray continually.

I THESSALONIANS 5:16–17

If I had my druthers, when my three children were growing up, I would have shielded them from all trouble. For them I would have cut teeth, bumped my head, skinned my knees, fought their fights, taken their heartaches, healed their relationships, handled their finances, suffered their pains, and guarded them from disappointments.

But life's not like that. People have to endure their own situations. Evidently, none of those problems did irreparable damage to my children. They turned out just fine. As I think about what would have happened if I had taken on their hurts, I can't help but say, "They sure would have made some stupid adults!" And I've learned that I should take their hurts to someone who can do something about them.

I remember one time when Vikki was in college and called home confused about her self-worth and her relationship with God. The questions she asked were perplexing to me; I didn't have adequate answers.

My heart was hurting because I didn't know what to say that would give her the encouragement she needed. So I prayed something like this, "Lord, I don't know how to pray for my child. I don't even understand how she got to this point. She was always self-confident, strong, and sure of you. Help me to help her. Please tell me what to do, what to say, how to respond to her. Father, I feel helpless!" The prayer continued for I don't know how long.

When I finished, I opened my eyes and saw a book on the shelf in front of me. It was Zig Ziglar's *See You at the Top*. I took that book and mailed it to Vikki even though I hadn't even read all of it and, at the time, didn't remember much of it. But I mailed it anyway, thinking possibly God would use it in her life.

A few days later, my child called and said, "Mama, thank you for sending me that book. It has literally changed by life. All the questions I had were answered."

I couldn't fix her hurt, but I could take her hurt to the One who knew how to bring healing, and he did it through a method I would never have guessed.

I've had similar times of intense prayer for my son and my other daughter. As a mother, I find solace in praying for my children during the good times and the bad. It's a fact, when our children are hurt or disappointed, confused or sad, we hurt too. I think we feel their emotions as deeply as they do.

To help my children and myself to get focused on how to deal with problems, I ask my children if they have listened to praise music before they called to tell me about their woes. Sometimes they have; sometimes they haven't. If they haven't, I ask them to call back after they have—unless, of course, it's an emergency.

I believe one of the best ways to get in a praying mood is to listen to music that ushers you into a spirit of adoration. That, in turn, takes your mind off the problem and helps you to focus on the Problem Solver. It brings harmony to your soul.

While I wait for them to call back, I follow my own instructions. I sing, listen to gospel music, and pray. Usually, when they phone me again, both of us are in harmony with each other and the Lord.

We are admonished to pray without ceasing because prayers assert God's power in our lives. When we fail to pray, we aren't cheating God; we're cheating ourselves. I like the following prayer because it reminds me that I can pray about anything:

Give me a good digestion, Lord,
And also something to digest;
Give me a healthy body, Lord,
With sense to keep it at its best.
Give me a healthy mind, Good Lord,
To keep the good and pure in sight,
Which, seeing sin, is not appalled
But finds a way to set it right.
Give me a mind that is not bored,
That does not whimper, whine, or sigh;
Don't let me worry over much
About the fussy thing called "I."
Give me a sense of humor, Lord,
Give me the grace to see a joke,
To get some pleasure out of life
And pass it on to other folk.

FROM THE REFECTORY
OF THE CATHEDRAL AT CHESTER, ENGLAND

Shielding our loved ones from the consequences of their problems often isn't possible. But praying for their ability to handle those problems is appropriate and can benefit them and us. If you're trying to accept responsibility for the problems of others, pray for them and pray with them—without ceasing.

"Father, you've made it possible for us to stay in contact with you all the time, wherever we are. Even our unuttered thoughts can be prayers, which enables us to pray without ceasing. Thank you for always being available and never on vacation. Thank you, also, for allowing the Holy Spirit to pray for us when we don't know how to pray. Amen."

FREEDOM FOR NOTHING

Marilyn Meberg

We have been released from the law so that
we serve in the new way of the Spirit,
and not in the old way of the written code.

ROMANS 7:6

One of my favorite activities in life is reading. As a child raised in rural communities with few libraries, I was thrilled when the bookmobile rolled into my area every other week. With my books strapped to the back carrier of my bike, I would eagerly pedal a little more than a mile to where the bookmobile was parked at the end of Williams Road. Happily fortified with new summer reading selections, I'd pedal back home, clamber up the makeshift ladder to my tree house, and settle in with my new book friends.

As an adult, most of my reading has been what I would call "meaningful." You know, life-enhancing, spirit-enlarging, or mind-expanding reading. But about a month ago, I experienced a throwback to the days of the bookmobile. Because of an unexpected and rather lengthy delay in a return flight from Dallas to Palm Springs, I wandered into an airport bookstore with the intention of picking up a pleasant "no-brainer" since I had finished reading everything I'd brought with me.

I stumbled onto a paperback that looked pleasant and would allow me to keep my pen in my purse. (Rarely can I read without a pen in hand because so often a word, sentence, or paragraph will be so terrific I have to underline it, make notes about it, or even talk back to the author in the margins.) This book appeared to be non-provocative but also non-boring, a great combination for the moment.

Several hours later, as we lurched onto the windswept runway in Palm Springs, I finished the book and smiled happily. "Marilyn," I said, "when was the last time you settled in for a mindlessly pleasant read? Why don't you do that more often? How come you feel you're wasting time if you're not reading Philip Yancey, Eugene Peterson, or Henri Nouwen? (Just for starters . . .) What's driving you continually to be productive? Have you forgotten those lazy afternoons in your tree house in which you just kicked back and floated where your book-inspired imagination took you?"

With an abruptness that matched the plane's grinding halt at the gate, it hit me that I had settled into some legalistic thinking about my reading habits. Unless my reading contributed to my spiritual or intellectual growth, I didn't take the time. I'd gotten a bit out of balance, and I suspected I'd been thinking that way for some time. What a loss!

I do gain much pleasure from reading meaningful material; it is not a grind or a chore. But not to allow myself any other kind of reading was unbalanced and a bit narrow.

In an effort to put myself back in balance, I've decided I will do enjoyable but mindless reading on airplanes only. This decision, however, has not proven to be problem free. On my last flight, I found myself uncomfortable reading *Uppity Women of Ancient Times* instead of *Healing Meditation for Life* because the flight attendant had attended one of our Joyful Journey conferences and benefited from it. I found myself camouflaging my book between the pages of *Today's Christian Woman* in case she should see my book title and think me shallow. At least I had the good sense to leave *Do Penguins Have Knees?* in my briefcase.

Perhaps some of you, like me, are missing out on recreational activity that has no purpose other than to give a needed respite from our task-oriented lives. Wouldn't it be fun occasionally to produce nothing, accomplish nothing, and contribute to nothing? Maybe that means reading a book that doesn't require a pen, or maybe it's a meander through the mall or a stroll (not a jog) through the park. The possibilities for nothing are endless.

"Lord Jesus, it's so liberating to know you love me for who I am and not for what I do. I have been set free from the laws that required me to perform to be acceptable to you. Now, because of Jesus, I am made perfect in spite of my imperfection. Teach me to rest and enjoy the life and the world you have placed me in. Restore my joy as I luxuriate in my freedom from the 'old way of the written code.' Amen."

BARKING UP THE WRONG ME

Patsy Clairmont

Look upon my affliction and rescue me.

PSALM 119:153 NASB

I have been doing the most ridiculous thing, and trust me it has not added one iota to my joy. I am baby-sitting. No, not for a chubby-cheeked, cooing cherub. I only wish that were the case. I am tending to a dog. No, not one that bounds about the house with frisky enthusiasm, for that actually would tickle me. It's not even an old pooch who agreeably curls up in the corner and snores. I'd probably join him. I could even deal with a snarling, chew-off-the-sofa-leg kind of mutt compared to this one.

Instead, my tend-ee is a virtual pet. Yep, you read it right. I'm jumping through cyberspace hoops, so to speak, trying to care for this unnamed, unclaimed, onscreen mongrel.

It all started when I saw these futuristic playmates dangling harmlessly from a wall in a small shop in my hometown. These items are pocketsize and conveniently attached to key chains.

We were going to visit our nephew Joshua, and I thought this would make a great gift for him. That was before I activated the computer-prompted pup.

On the long drive to Joshua's (540 miles), I decided I would figure out how this pet operated so I could teach Josh. I opened the package, started the action, then leaned back to read the fine print. Well, 350 miles later I was still trying to understand the directions. (The manufacturer's tape that partially covered the instructions didn't help. But I'm not sure I would have understood even if all the info were available to me.)

Because I didn't "get it," the dad-blamed gadget kept beeping at me. I understood enough to realize when it beeped it was signaling me to do something for this animated animal. But what, pray tell, was I to do?

I learned along our travels that once activated I was responsible for this dog's longevity (talk about a load). This meant if I didn't tend to it in a timely and correct manner, the pup would leave home and cease to exist. Talk about a guilt trip.

The first night before reaching our destination, Les and I stayed at a motel. All evening the little hand-held machine tweeted repeatedly, summoning me. At first its little pleas for help fed my codependent heart, and I merrily tried to figure out which buttons to push to care for its needs. But, as the evening wore on, my nerves wore thin with the insistent shrill beeping. Even irritated, though, I continued to care for my charge, thinking I'd soon hand him over to Josh. Talk about a misconception.

By the time we arrived the following day, I realized this pet was too complex for young Joshua. Well, then I'd just have to find someone older to give it to, I assured myself. Think again. No one wanted, needed, or desired the pipsqueak.

For days I walked around with this neurotic aggravation tucked in my pocket, making demands on my life.

Have you ever seen one of these pesky pets? If not, listen up. You have to feed the pup, bathe him, give him shots, discipline him, play catch with him, put him to bed, and clean up his smelly deposits. C'mon, that's more than I'm willing to do for my husband. If that's not enough, this mutt-machine has a report card that grades how well you're doing and how pleased your pet is with your behavior.

That was the final straw. A report card, why, that's ludicrous. If you think I'm lugging this yapping thing through life then think again!

Think? Hmm, think.

Perhaps that's what I should have done to begin with—put a little more purchasing thought into my decision.

Have you made any hasty decisions lately? Are they causing you unnecessary pressure? What can you do about it? What kind of a decision-making report card would you give yourself?

"Lord, how often do we lose our joy over something we got ourselves into? Thank you that you do rescue us and that you grade us mercifully. Amen."

I REMEMBER IT WELL

Luci Swindoll

Remember the wonders he has done,
his miracles, and the judgments.
1 CHRONICLES 16:12

I'm a hunter. My weapon is a camera, and I keep it loaded. In fact, five minutes ago, while going from one room to the other, I spotted a hawk on my patio, perched on the back of a chair. It's never been there before and may never be again. So, very quietly, I picked up my weapon with its 400mm zoom lens, crawled down the hallway, started to shoot, and clicked off maybe ten rounds on that single target. What a moment!

Two days ago, I picked off three hot-air balloons whooshing over my house. A month ago I shot the liftoff of the space shuttle Atlantis, and earlier this summer, I managed several close-up photos in a butterfly sanctuary.

I've snapped pictures of whales, wild animals in the bush, cat fights, foreign cities, autumn leaves, great horned owls, parties, weddings, children playing, lightning, snowfalls, family, friends, strangers. Many are framed and adorn my house. I consider almost every moment a "Kodak moment," to borrow a phrase. Why, I hardly go to the corner without my camera. What if I miss something? I couldn't stand it. Wherever I go, I'm in search of a memory.

I've journaled for many years in part because I want to remember meaningful times and people dear to me. I treasure these volumes more and more, and I count on them to reveal everything as it actually happened. They are a concise chronicle of my life.

In September, I turned sixty-five. One of my dearest friends gave me a memory book called "Remember When." She sent fifty blank pages to family members and friends and asked them to surprise me with the account of a time they remembered with me. There was a place to write and a spot to include a photo. I can't tell you what that gift means to me. When I opened it, I cried like a baby. The memories floated off those pages as my mind went a hundred different directions. It's a wonderful book. Maybe the best gift I've ever received.

And guest books? Let me tell you about those! I have the writings of my mom and dad (both now with the Lord), accounts of parties and holidays, and thank-you notes from countless friends. Each page is a wonderful memory captured on paper. Those books take me back to times of great joy.

Remembering is important to God. He encourages us to make memories. In Joshua 3–4, we read the account of the Israelites moving the ark of the covenant across the flooded Jordan River. After the water parted to allow the ark and the Israelites to cross, God commanded the leaders of the twelve tribes to take one stone each from the river and to place it where the priests had stood with the ark when they arrived safely on the other shore. "These stones are to be a memorial to the people of Israel forever" (Joshua 4:7). A stack of stones, believed to be the original one, stands on the bank of the Jordan today!

Scripture is replete with verses on remembering. We're encouraged to remember days of old, the wonders of God, the Sabbath, God's deeds and our struggles, our Creator, our youth, and that life is short. On and on the commands to remember go.

If you've not yet begun to create memories, start now. Load up your camera with film, fill that pen with ink, and capture the miracles and wonders that come your way. Surround yourself with whatever it takes to be reminded. God is faithful. Don't ever forget that.

"Lord, help me to remember all the ways you lead me, bless me, keep me. May I be a repository of those memories and be quick to share them with others. They are the proof of your constant faithfulness. Thank you. Amen."

STORM WARNING

Sheila Walsh

A quarrelsome wife is like
a constant dripping on a rainy day.

PROVERBS 27:15

Barry and I lay in bed one night in a hotel watching television. When the *Mary Tyler Moore Show* was over, we switched off the TV and settled in to sleep. There it was: *drip! drip! drip!* One of us hadn't completely switched off the bathroom tap. I knew Barry wasn't sleeping yet so I burrowed under the covers, waiting for him to get up and turn it off. Instead, he turned over and dug in deep, too.

"Can't you hear that tap?" I asked.

"Yep, I sure can," he replied. "That's a tap all right!"

I lay there for about ten minutes, determined not to get out of my cozy bed. But I felt as if I were being tortured by Nazis!

"All right, all right!" I cried. "I surrender." I leapt out of bed and turned off the offending lethal weapon, at which point Barry said, "Oh, thanks! That was kind of bugging me."

Is there anything in the Bible about not smothering your husband with a pillow?

Afterwards, I decided it was time to pay a visit to a wise and godly counselor I know. "Life can be so great, and then out of the blue I get mad over some stupid little thing," I told him. "I hate who I am in those moments."

"Have you asked God to help you?" he asked me.

"Well, to be honest, Scott," I continued, "I don't feel like talking to God when I'm as mad as that."

"But that's when you need to," he said.

A few days passed, and I didn't think much more about my conversation with Scott. In fact, I was in such a good mood, I decided God must have answered my prayers and my drip was permanently dried up. Then ...

"Did you mail that insurance form, sweetie?" I asked Barry one afternoon, knowing he had because we had talked about how important it was.

He seemed to lose a little color. He looked at me, he looked at the door, he lifted his eyes to heaven. "I forgot," he said.

"Why would you forget something as important as that?" I asked, feeling some of the old emotions rising.

"I'm sorry, honey. I just forgot," he said.

I found myself standing on the edge of a cliff and knew I had to choose whether I would dive off or back off. I asked Barry to excuse me for a moment, and I went upstairs to our bedroom.

"Lord, what do I do here?" I cried. "I'm angry. Please help me."

At that moment, I made a conscious, determined choice to get on my knees and to let my anger go. As I released my fury, I was filled with joy.

I heard Barry's footsteps on the stairs. When he came into the room looking like he knew he had really blown it, I could honestly say, "It doesn't matter. We can sort this out tomorrow."

Choosing to let go of my tempestuous responses may not seem big to you, but it's making a huge difference in our lives. I want to be the fragrance of Christ in the midst of the storms of life, not part of the storm front. I still blow it sometimes, but I'm catching myself more quickly, and I ask Barry to forgive me. I want to be a blessing to my husband. I want him to look forward to coming home, not dread bumping into the rainy day in blue jeans.

If you struggle with old behaviors that are as familiar to you as the spider veins on your legs, I encourage you to invite Christ into the moment and to let those old patterns go. It's not easy, but it's right. You can choose. You can be a drip of rain or a ray of sunshine.

"Lord, help me to let your light into my darkness,
Your love into my unloveliness,
Your grace into my smallness.
Amen."

LET'S FACE IT

Marilyn Meberg

I can do everything through him who gives me strength.

PHILIPPIANS 4:13

When Ken and I first moved to Laguna Beach, California, I was excited about walking the beach each morning as my exercise routine. I saw it as an exhilarating way to stay fit, to talk to the Lord, and to revel in my surroundings.

One morning, about three weeks into my daily reveling, I was making my way down to Main Beach when I noticed over my right shoulder what looked like a Doberman trotting some distance behind me. I had no reason to be alarmed, but I was the only one on the beach, and the dog was not on a leash. That made me a tad nervous. After all, Dobermans are known to be fierce guard dogs. Maybe he felt the need to fiercely guard the beach. I picked up my pace. So did he!

Looking edgily over my shoulder, I noticed the dog was gaining on me. He wasn't running, but he was doing what I'd call a fast trot. I, too, broke into a fast trot. That seemed to encourage him to increase his speed, so I increased mine. Within a short time, I was moving at a full-on run. So was he. I began to huff and puff. As the dog continued to gain on me, I envisioned newspaper headlines, "Middle-aged woman with nostrils full of sand found facedown, dead from a massive heart attack." Or "Woman's shredded remains found scattered along the sands of Laguna Beach, unidentified dog sitting close by with blue sweatshirt threads dangling from mouth."

I didn't like either of those headlines, yet I knew within moments he would be upon me. So I abruptly stopped running and turned to face him. He was delighted. He came bounding up to me, tail wagging and obviously eager to be petted. I stroked his face and neck and then dropped onto the sand with exhaustion and relief. To his obvious delight I scratched his ears and told him what a fright he had given me. He didn't seem to comprehend anything other than that he had made a new friend. Together then, we ultimately arrived at Main Beach, with his stopping repeatedly to wait for me.

I have metaphorically applied that story to my life many times. For instance, I have envisioned certain fears that I kept trying to keep ahead of, only to find that when I stopped and faced them, there really was nothing to fear after all. What I needed to do was quit trying to avoid them and face them instead.

After my husband died, I didn't think I could handle money matters like taxes, interest rates, and investments. After all, I have a number phobia. No one with a number phobia can figure out and keep track of stuff more complex than the price of broccoli, cauliflower, and grapefruit. I had no choice but to turn and face that fear. I would still rather deal with investments like broccoli, cauliflower, and grapefruit, but I have learned it won't leave me dead on the beach to read a tax form.

Dashing ahead of the Dobermans of life leaves me breathless and scared. Facing them with a prayer on my lips and faith in my heart allows me not only to trust God more but also to experience victory that comes from no one but him. Actually, that is a rather exhilarating way to stay fit.

"Father, thank you that my ability to face down my inadequacies and fears comes from your promise that I can do everything through you. Thank you for the exhilaration of seeing and feeling your strength working in me. I am grateful. Amen."

GOD'S MOUTHPIECE

Thelma Wells

At the name of Jesus every knee should bow,
in heaven and on earth and under the earth,
and every tongue confess that Jesus Christ is Lord,
to the glory of God the Father.

PHILIPPIANS 2:10–11

My husband, George, and I vacationed once with another couple in New Orleans. One day we spent four hours walking from the hotel to the end of the French Market, stopping to eat, shop, listen to jazz, watch a human mannequin, and observe the activities of this Cajun city.

After we had walked so far, all of us voted to take a taxi back to the hotel. So we flagged a cab. While the driver ate lunch and asked us where we were from, he drove us to our destination. His priorities seemed to be in that order: eat, talk, drive.

My friends told him they were from Houston, and George and I said we were from Dallas. The driver, in between bites of his sandwich, said, "I'm from Palestine. Do you know where Palestine is? It's where my people are fighting with the Jews because they have stolen our land."

His statements opened a path to an interesting and disturbing conversation. I asked him if the fighting over there was a continuation of the differences between Ishmael and Isaac. He replied, "No, the fighting started in 1948 when the Jews came back and stole our land."

"Do you think there will ever be peace in the Middle East?" I asked.

He replied, "Not until we kick them out and get our land back." He continued to explain about his people and their enemies, the Jews, and he moved on to crunching an apple.

The conversation then slid into a discussion of religion. He proudly told us he was a Muslim, and as a Muslim he believed in God. I wanted to know how he felt about Muhammad. He indicated Muhammad was a good guy just like Jesus. He didn't believe God had a Son. His reasoning was, "If God had one son, why didn't he have a daughter or a mother?"

That question didn't make sense to me, but I wasn't going to let that stop me from commenting. So I leapfrogged to a point I wanted to make. "Believing in Jesus happens in your heart by faith. I believe in Jesus Christ. I believe in the Trinity. What do you know about the Holy Spirit?"

Now it was his turn to be perplexed. Evidently he had never heard of the Holy Spirit. I was just warming up to the subject when, wouldn't you know it, we arrived at our hotel. Mr. Taxi Driver practically drove up on the curb and then opened the door with such energy, I thought it was going to come off the hinges. I wasn't sure if he was always that exuberant or if he was just happy to see this group of "Holy Spirit" people leaving his car.

Even after he dropped us off, my thoughts about the conversation continued. I rehearsed my statements and wondered what else I could have done to witness to the driver. What could I have said to show him that the way to get to God is through his only Son, Jesus? I realized I hadn't known enough about the Muslim religion to respond adequately to the issues Mr. T. Driver raised in our discussion. The more I thought about it, the heavier my heart became.

Then I remembered one of God's promises: that his Word would not return to him void. I could have used Scripture to help the Palestinian understand what I was saying. Several verses came to my mind even then.

Ultimately, I didn't gain perspective on that conversation until I reminded myself that if the fellow had accepted what I said and chose Jesus as his Savior right there in the taxi (hallelujah!), I couldn't have taken credit. God draws people to himself. Each of us is just his mouthpiece on earth.

Whether we say just the right thing or can't think of anything that seems right, all we can do is open our mouths and trust God to use us. That doesn't mean we shouldn't be prepared to offer a reasoned explanation for our faith, but it does take the pressure off of us. We are the instruments, but God is the one who must make the music through us.

After the taxi conversation, I asked God to forgive me for not adequately explaining who Jesus is. I asked God to speak to the driver's heart and to draw him to the Lord despite my muffed attempt. This prayer made me feel a lot better.

Have you tried to explain a spiritual principle to someone lately and sounded only sour notes? Have you been stymied about how to make clear that which seems so obvious to you? Remembering your role and God's role can help to comfort you if you've blown it and give you the push you may need to increase your knowledge so you can "sound off" more eloquently next time.

"Master, as one of your mouthpieces on this earth, I realize that sometimes you give me opportunities to talk about you that I blow. How grateful I am that when I miss my chance, you (I'm sure) have someone else you will use to draw that person to you. That doesn't get me off the hook, but it sure takes the pressure off. Teach me more about how to tell others about you. Amen."

SAY "CHEESE"

Patsy Clairmont

See, I have engraved you
on the palms of my hands.

ISAIAH 49:16

Picture this: years of photographic debris littered hither and yon; some photos crammed in drawers, taped on mirrors, stacked on desks, magnetized to the refrigerator, stuffed in shoe boxes, propped against window frames, crinkled up in purses, pressed in old books, mixed in with the bills.... This is indicative of how for years I have handled our family's pictorial history.

I've always meant to organize, alphabetize, and categorize these frames of life, but I'm not naturally organizational, alphabetical, or categorical. In fact, I'm more eclectic in my approach to life. Some might say I'm a willy-nilly, helter-skelter, or if-you-can-find-it-you-can-have-it kind of a person. Now, don't get me wrong; I like a tidy environment. Just don't open a door or drawer without taking some precautions. That is, if you can yank them open and then force them closed again. But if you do pry open a drawer, would you mind seeing if you could find the three rolls of film I misplaced from our family vacation, summer 1992? I know they are here somewhere.

I also know I need to get a grip on our photos. So I took the following action. First, I conducted a pictorial roundup. All floaters were brought into the living room and put inside Les's grandfather's trunk that presides in front of our couch. This activity actually took weeks, as we rooted around retrieving wayward pictures from strange and unusual locations (medicine cabinet, toolbox, clothes dryer).

Once the majority had been packed into the trunk, I purchased albums of all sizes. Then I sat down in front of the mountainous heap, and in a brief time became overwhelmed with this wide-load project. I couldn't figure out how to separate them into categories. Should it be by years, events, houses, individuals, vacations, celebrations, crises, or all of the above?

Actually, I couldn't even figure out who some of these folks were. I mean, who in the world let these strangers into our house? Like the guy with the cigar and the big schnozzola. Where did he come from? Or the woman in the tattered flapper dress swinging a hula hoop around her doughy midsection? (Oops, never mind; that's me in my nightgown.) And who are all these babies? Portly babies, pining babies, puckered babies, peaceful babies. Why, I could start a pediatrics ward—or an orphanage, since their names remain a mystery.

This brings me to my next dilemma: How does one toss out a picture without guilt? A person's likeness is so personal it seems like a violation to discard them. After all, what if these individuals have rejection issues?

Les and I were in an antique shop the other day when we spotted a photo album on a table. Interested, we peeked inside only to find a family peering back at us.

We both felt sad seeing someone's snapshots cast aside for strangers to peruse. We wondered who would throw away his or her history (a few family members maybe, but the whole clan)? And who would purpose to buy more relatives?

Gradually, I'm making progress with the development of our albums and have in courageous moments thrown out a few strangers (not the cigar man; I've bonded with him). I've even parted with a myriad of duplicates. (I had forty-seven outside shots of one of our homes. Perhaps my finger stuck, or the camera was new, or my hot flashes and the camera flashes were in competition—who knows? I've thinned them down to twenty-nine.)

My eighty-three-year-old mom recently condensed her life, and guess what she gave me . . . a chestful of unidentified photographs. Yikes! Back to searching for identity clues.

Ever feel like your identity is lost in a world full of people? We have a God whose heart is expansive enough to hold us all and yet who's so intently focused on each of us that he knows our rising up and our sitting down.

Meditate on Psalm 139. Then smile pretty; heaven's watching.

"Dear Lord, thank you that you are a God of order and that you never lose track of us. We are comforted to know that once we're in your family we will never be discarded. It fills us with joy realizing you have framed us with your love and view us through your mercy. Our faces are no surprise to you, Lord, and our identities are engraved in the palms of your hands. (Whew.) Amen."

LET MAMA OUT OF THE TRUNK

Sheila Walsh

Listen to your father, who gave you life,
and do not despise your mother when she is old.

Proverbs 23:22

A friend of mine recently told me he now only talks to his mother by e-mail because it makes her more bearable. I asked him if he had ever discussed with her the difficulty they had communicating. He looked at me as if I had suggested he stick his hand in a blender. "You've got to be kidding," he said. "Talk to my mother? That's like trying to bargain with a scorpion!"

Since I've become a mother, I have a new appreciation for my own mom. When I realized what labor pains were all about, I wanted to buy her a small country! I now know, in such a deeper way, that the parent and the child are irrevocably part of the tapestry of each other's lives. How sad to try to ignore a part of that tapestry or "endure" its presence.

Why do we find it so hard at times to relate to our mothers, to speak the truth to those who gave us life? When I say "speak the truth," I mean loving, ongoing truth, not a stream of "I'm a jerk because you dropped me when I was two" accusations.

Part of the problem is we don't talk honestly to each other in our families. We feel guilty if we have negative feelings toward our parents. So we stuff those feelings and then wish we could stuff our parents! True love demands a different approach: honesty, taking risks with one another, and enduring some difficult moments because we want a real relationship.

One of the most freeing moments in my relationship with my mother was when I realized I wasn't responsible for her emotional well-being or happiness. I used to have an inflated sense of responsibility and wandered around for years like a demented nurse taking every family member's emotional temperature. But I quit my job. It was too exhausting, and I'm sure I was annoying.

In case you're stuck in that role with your family, especially with your mother, I offer this suggestion: Date your mother. Now, before you think I've taken a permanent dive off the wagon of sanity, let me explain. When you first began to date your husband or pursued a new relationship with a potential friend, you gave it all you had. You asked questions because you were hungry to know more about this person. You listened, and as trust and mutual respect grew, you shared your hopes and dreams with that person.

Our mothers had lives before we came along. But often we know very little about that young woman with hopes and dreams of her own who would lie awake at night and wonder how her life would turn out. Finding out who that woman is and was can be fascinating, just like discovering a new friend.

Often family members behave in set patterns simply because that's what we expect each other to do. It's a dance that has developed over the years between us. So take a fresh look. Put on a new record. Get to know your mother in ways you haven't before. Celebrate the woman she is. Say "thank you." Send her flowers. Write her a note. Take her out to dinner. Buy her something she wanted as a child and never got. Take a good look. Move a little closer. And let Mama out of the trunk!

"Dear Lord, today I want to thank you for my mother. Thank you for all the thankless moments she endured from me and went on loving anyway. Thank you for her time and patience and forgiveness. Help me to find new ways to express my love to her. In your name and grace, Amen."

FILL 'ER UP

Refueling Your Soul

WHO DO YOU BE?

Marilyn Meberg

Before I formed you in the womb I knew you,
before you were born I set you apart;
I appointed you as a prophet to the nations.

JEREMIAH 1:5

My grandson Ian bequeathed upon me a most unusual name when he was about fifteen months old. The name is "Maungya." We are unaware of its origins other than that it sprung from this little fellow's fertile mind.

I love the name. Lots of Grandmas, Grannys, and Nanas populate the world, but to my knowledge, there are no Maungyas. That name sets me apart, makes me unique. He calls his daddy's mother "Nana" and my daughter Beth's biological mother "Nana Sherry," but my designation is like no other.

During my last visit, just the two of us were playing in his sandbox. I was sifting the sand through a sieve in an effort to eliminate the ground cover bark that had managed to get into the mix and annoyed me slightly.

My intensity for this task was intruded upon by an unexpected question from Ian. "Maungya, who do you be?"

Noting the seriousness of his big blue eyes, I felt compelled to answer the question seriously but found myself at a loss for words. Quoting Ephesians 1:4, that I was one chosen before the foundation of the world to "be," seemed a bit theological for the moment. Telling him that Jeremiah 1:5 says I was known even in the womb and designed to "be" also seemed a bit heavy.

I opted for saying, "Maungya is your grandma."

"I know," he said with slight irritation.

"And," I continued, realizing I hadn't answered well yet, "God made her to love you really, really big just like God loves Ian really, really big."

At this, Ian discontinued putting the bark back in the sandbox that I had managed to sift out and stared off into space. Quietly, he repeated, "Maungya loves Ian really, really big." After a few more seconds he said, "God loves Ian really, really big."

Seemingly satisfied, he said, "Yeah, yup," an expression he used to indicate agreement as well as finality on whatever subject is being discussed.

We then resumed our futile take-the-bark-out, put-the-bark-back activity with renewed camaraderie.

I, of course, have pondered this little exchange ever since. The question of "who do you be, who do I be" is foundational to all of us. We want and need to know who we are. I'm just a bit stunned that Ian is giving it thought already.

The question is asked in Lewis Carroll's *Alice in Wonderland*, "Who in the world am I? Ah, that's the great puzzle!" But, of course, for the believer, there need not be a puzzle. Referring back to Jeremiah 1:5, I learn who "I be."

To begin with, I was in God's mind before I was ever in the womb of my mother. The phrase, "Before I formed you in the womb I knew you" is mind-boggling. Specific attention, thought, and planning about me took place before God actually formed me in the womb. That implies I am much more than a cozy encounter between my parents nine months before I was born. No matter the circumstances surrounding my conception, I am a planned event.

Not only am I a planned event, I was "set apart," called or given to be a "prophet to the nations." I, like Jeremiah, have a specific task to do for God. We all have a specific task to do for God, and it was planned in his head before we were ever formed in the womb. That is an incredible truth!

Not only is my identity and calling known, but also Isaiah 43:1 says, "I have called you by name, you are mine" (RSV). I can't imagine God calling me "Maungya," but I do know that like that name, he considers me unique and set apart, and he calls me his own. I can't wait to tell all this to Ian in a few more years. I suppose by then there will be only bark in the sandbox.

"Lord Jesus, the knowledge that each of us is a unique, made-to-order creation whom you love, whom you call by name, and for whom you have a plan is security-producing. May we sink into that cushion of joyful peace and never forget 'whose we be.' Amen."

BRAND SPANKING NEW

Patsy Clairmont

Put on the new self.

EPHESIANS 4:24

When I stopped by my friends Gene and Ruthann Bell's home, I had no idea a miracle had just occurred on their premises. Ruthann proudly led me down their wooded lane and through the barn. Then she opened the large wooden door into the back barnyard. There, standing next to his stately mother, Mariah (a registered Morgan), was a wee colt.

Christened Huw (Welsh spelling for "Hugh" and named for the character Huw Morgan in *How Green Was My Valley*, a Welsh novel), the five-hour-old newborn teetered and tottered on his spindly legs. He eyed us with caution as he leaned in closer to his mom. Then, when Mariah moved into the open corral, the colt tried to scamper after her. His knobby legs kept tangling up on him. We laughed the kind of sweet laughter that comes from taking delight in the wonders of new life.

What pleasure I found in observing this bony bundle toddling, testing his unpolished prance, trying out his touchy brakes while never straying far from his mother. The colt instinctively knew to nuzzle in to her for nourishment, comfort, and protection.

Ever wish you could start over? Probably all of us have longed for another chance in some area of our lives. We wouldn't necessarily have done things differently, just more or perhaps less. For starters I wish I would have read more when I was in school (when I could still retain), and I wish I had griped less when I was a young mom.

The truth is we can't go back, only forward into uncharted territory. To sit in our sorrow would lead to misery. Although regret that leads to change is a dear friend, regret that leads to shame is a treacherous enemy.

So how do we live without allowing regret to rob us of our joy? How about this insight to prompt us on: "And lean not on your own understanding" (Proverbs 3:5).

Sometimes we are so certain we know something, when, dear sisters, we don't really. Know what I mean? There is no guarantee that if we had done a part of our lives differently things would end up any different. We have to trust the God of the universe who directs the outcome of all things that he will do that which ultimately needs to be done (in spite of us, if necessary).

I'm not suggesting we don't need to take responsibility for past mistakes or that we shouldn't learn to do things more honorably, for these are changes that lead to fresh beginnings. But I am saying many things are now out of our control but never his.

So next time you and I need something to lean on, let's make it the Lord. Then we can nuzzle in and receive what we need most—nourishment from his Word, comfort from his Spirit, and the protection of his presence.

Leaning in also offers us the benefit of no regrets and an opportunity to "put on the new self."

"Lord, thank you that as we lean into you for nourishment, comfort, and protection (fill 'er up), we then can enter into our fresh beginnings (new day, job, resolve) with enthusiasm. May it delight you, Lord, to see us toddle and sometimes prance in our efforts, and may it even cause you to throw back your head and laugh with sweet abandon. Amen."

DON'T TAKE MY WORD FOR IT

Luci Swindoll

I know your deeds, that you are neither cold nor hot.
I wish you were either one or the other! So,
because you are lukewarm—neither hot nor cold
—I am about to spit you out of my mouth.

REVELATION 3:15–16

A hillbilly walked into a novelty store. He saw a shiny thermos and asked the clerk what it was. The clerk replied, "It's a thermos. It keeps cold things cold and hot things hot." The hillbilly was so impressed he bought one.

He couldn't wait to show it off to his friends. At work the next day, he didn't have to wait long before one of his peers asked him what that shiny thing was.

The hillbilly replied, "It's a thermos. It keeps cold things cold and hot things hot."

His coworker asked him, "Well, what do you have in it now?"

The hillbilly proudly replied, "A Popsicle and two cups of coffee!"

I'm with the hillbilly. I like cold things cold, and hot things hot with no in-between. I'm all or nothing. I know what I like and what I don't. As a Southerner, I can eat my weight in fried okra but don't feed me hominy. An as opera lover, I'd lay down my life for Puccini's music but deliver me from Alban Berg. As a moviegoer, give me a sit-on-the-edge-of-my-chair psychological thriller but do not make me wade through some sappy, boy-meets-girl, girl-wears-cute-clothes, boy-marries-girl, couple-has-baby. Please!

You don't have to agree with me. It's often more fun when you don't; it sparks great conversation. I've worked for years to develop these opinions, and they define me.

That's one thing I love about Marilyn. She has her own thoughts, states her preferences, holds to her convictions, and when we differ, she doesn't try to change my mind. She lets me be me.

For instance, I love the Old Country Buffet restaurant in Palm Desert (where we both live), but Marilyn loathes it. The food caters to home-style cooking, honors senior citizen discounts, and one can go back to the trough as often as desired. It's inexpensive, all-you-can-eat, come-as-you-are. My kind of place! But Marilyn? No, thanks! If I want to go there, I have to find another hillbilly. Marilyn's opinion doesn't keep me from going; it just keeps me from going with her.

I remember a friend in my bygone days who could never make up her mind.

I'd ask, "Want to go to dinner?"

"It doesn't matter," she would say.

"Okay, let's go out. Afterward, how 'bout a movie?"

"Whatever you say."

"What would you like to see?"

"Whatever . . ."

That drove me crazy! I didn't mind deciding, but I never had the chance to know her. Of course, she didn't know herself.

Our choices validate us. They tell us who we are and convey to others where we stand. By not having personal convictions, my friend lacked strength of character. She went through life neither hot nor cold.

This becomes a serious problem when you go beyond music, movies, or meals to important issues like faith. I'm talking about a mind-set, a disposition toward life wherein Jesus Christ is your center, his Word is your standard, and his way your choice.

God requires a person to make choices—to be hot or cold, to know what you believe and why. I'm not suggesting we hold stubbornly or unreasonably to our own opinions. However, when it comes to biblical convictions or spiritual truth, we must take a stand. Wisdom, peace, courage, and joy characterize the people I know who do.

"Father, help us make choices that please you. We don't want to be weak or stubborn. We want to be right on. Like you. Amen."

DELIGHTFULLY DECEIVED

Barbara Johnson

Do not forget to entertain strangers, for by so doing some people have entertained angels without knowing it.

HEBREWS 13:2

Our youngest son, Barney, was planning a surprise party for his wife, Shannon, at a hotel in San Diego, and he invited Bill and me to join the fun. On a lark, we decided to take the train, and we invited my friend Lynda along.

After our train arrived, we jostled our carry-on bags into the train station, expecting Barney to be waiting for us on the platform. All the other passengers scurried around as we stood there, scanning the crowd for Barney's handsome face. But he wasn't there.

We shuffled our things over to a bench to wait. Gradually, the large waiting area emptied, and we were alone. I dug through my purse for a quarter and the number of the hotel where we were supposed to stay. The only pay phone in sight was way off in the corner, and as Lynda and I walked toward it, a disheveled man leaning against the wall raised his head and watched us.

From beneath a tattered baseball cap, his long, scraggly, black hair fell over his eyes and hung in tangles. His stained and wrinkled trousers were four sizes too big. One part of his ragged shirttail hung outside his sagging waistband while the rest was loosely stuffed inside. His canvas shoes were as holey as Swiss cheese. Little clouds of smoke rose out of the cigarette that dangled from his mouth.

My heart lurched a little at the unexpected sight, and Lynda must have been startled by the man's appearance, too, because she reached for my arm and said, "Barb . . ." as she made a frightened face.

"Just imagine," I told her, patting her hand reassuringly, "that poor man is someone's kid."

I made the call, only to find Barney wasn't at the hotel. "I guess we'll just have to wait. He probably got stopped for another traffic ticket."

As soon as I sat on the bench, the disheveled man slowly ambled toward us.

"Barb, he's coming toward us!" Lynda gasped, scooting closer to me on the bench.

"No, he's not," I hissed back, turning my head and pretending to look the other way while noting his every move out of the corner of my eye.

"He is! He's gonna rob us!" Lynda's lips didn't move, but her words were distinct.

The man's hands were in his pockets, and he was staring at us as he drew nearer.

I began to shuffle through my purse, trying to decide whether to offer him a couple of dollars—or a breath mint. Bill, engrossed in a magazine, was oblivious to the unfolding drama. I elbowed him, causing him to turn to me impatiently. "What?" he said too loudly.

The man was now less than ten feet away from us, and my heart was pounding. Lynda squirmed next to me on the bench, and the three of us sat there huddled together, watching the ragged man come nearer. Suddenly he spoke.

"Hi, Mom!"

Mom? If I wore dentures, they would have clattered to the floor. I stared at the man, who stood so close to me now I could look up under the bill of the baseball cap and peer into those twinkling dark eyes, those suddenly familiar eyes . . .

"Barney, it's you! What on earth . . . ?"

Now he was laughing so hard he couldn't talk. Wordlessly, he lifted off the cap—and the long, scraggly, black hair came off with it, a wig attached to the cap. The cigarette was fake, too; it emitted clouds of powder rather than smoke whenever Barney puffed on it. With a smile as wide as the Mississippi, he hitched up his enormous trousers while pulling me into his arms for a hug. Still feeling a little bewildered, I suddenly regretted all those tricks I had played on my family during our boys' growing-up years. Now, I realized, it was payback time.

Since that moment, I have developed a new empathy for how poor old Isaac must have felt when his conniving son Jacob showed up at Isaac's bedside disguised as his older brother, Esau. And I have a new understanding of the Scripture passage that says, "Can a mother forget her little child and not have love for her own son? Yet even if that should be, I will not forget you" (Isaiah 49:15 TLB).

Even when we're so low down and hard up our own mothers wouldn't recognize us, God sees through our disguises. He looks into our hearts and calls us his own.

"Dear Lord, you have promised not to forget me, even when I foolishly disguise myself in the ways of the world. Thank you for always remembering me and welcoming me back into your everlasting arms. Amen."

TAKE A FLYING LEAP

Sheila Walsh

Perfect love drives out fear.

1 JOHN 4:18

A woman at a conference recently asked me, "What does it look like to trust God?" I thought the question was wonderful. We talk about faith, trust, and love as easily as we talk about bread, milk, and eggs. But what do we really mean? What flesh do we hang on the bones of our words? Have you ever asked yourself what it looks like to trust God?

For me, it looks like Barbara Johnson. If you talk to any of us at Women of Faith about Barbara, we'll all tell you the same thing: The woman is amazing! I can't imagine the pain she has endured in her life. I can't comprehend the agony of identifying two dead sons. When Barbara tells her story on stage, I still weep as she uses the phrase "identify your first-born son in a box." I can't take it in. I can't bear to think about it.

But in the midst of the pain of her life, Barbara continues to pray, "Whatever, Lord." And her life of relinquishment to God has touched millions of people. She is grace and love in a purple dress. Barbara has grasped what George Fox said so eloquently, "And when all my hopes in them and in all men were gone, so that I had nothing outwardly to help me, nor could tell what to do, then, oh then, I heard a voice which said, 'There is one, even Christ Jesus, that can speak to thy condition,' and when I heard it my heart did leap for joy."

How can Barbara keep smiling and spreading joy across the world with so many arrows in her soul? Does it sound a little too head-in-the-sand to you? It's really not. The greatest fears of humankind are that we have no significance, that we are not loved, and that we will live and die alone. As Christians, we have those covered. No matter who you are, you are made in God's image. Your life has eternal significance through Christ. Even in the most stable relationships at times we can't be there for each other. But Christ will always be there. You are loved more than you can ever hope to comprehend. Christ is with you today as he was yesterday and will be tomorrow, and when you lay your head down for the last time, your life will be just beginning.

Barbara has grabbed hold of the gospel, the plain, simple truth. That's not head-in-the-sand, that's hands-in-the-air! Jesus hasn't come to fill your life with stuff; he's come to fill you with himself. It's not "out there." He's "in here." We aren't called to walk around with our fingers in our ears singing la-la-la-la-la, hoping the sky won't fall. Christian faith is never without content. Frances Schaefer said that Christian faith is never a jump in the dark. Christian faith always believes what God has said. And Christian faith rests on Christ's finished work on the cross.

It's because of who Barbara is trusting that she is not afraid.

Where do you find yourself today? Perhaps you are worried about a child who has wandered away from God, and fear grips your heart for him or her. Perhaps you look at a pile of bills and a fragile balance in your checkbook, and fear squeezes tight.

How can you look like Barbara Johnson? How can you trust? I encourage you to take a leap into the arms of the One who is able to fill your heart with love. Christ did not come to remove all our troubles but to walk with us through every one of them. So, take a leap. Take a flying leap!

"Lord Jesus,
Thank you that I can trust you.
Help me to trust you more.
I ask you to flood my heart with your love as I leap into your arms.
In your name I pray,
Amen."

MY SHEPHERD

Thelma Wells

The LORD is my Shepherd,
I shall not be in want.

PSALM 23:1

Most of the time when I say grace before a meal I say with conviction, "The LORD is my Shepherd, I shall not want!" Not because it's a short verse, which lets me feed my face sooner than saying a prayer, but because I really mean it.

When I say "The LORD is my Shepherd," I remember that he is my Savior, Master, Sovereign, All in All. He has charge over my life. As my Shepherd, he watches over me to see that I stay in the fold. He loves me unconditionally in spite of my going my own willful way sometimes. He protects me from danger. He provides everything for me. He chastises me when I do wrong. He comforts me when I am distressed. He bandages my wounds when I get hurt. He calms my fears when I am afraid. He takes care of my relationships when they become shaky. He bathes me in his Spirit when I seek his face. He communicates with me in ways I can understand.

"I shall not be in want." Now, that reminds me that I desire certain things: new draperies, new carpeting, new furniture. These are luxuries, not necessities, because I already have these things. I just want different ones. Know what I mean? God promises to provide all our *needs* according to his riches in glory in Christ Jesus. I know he will do that. And he delights in often giving us what we want as well.

I'm reminded of the time I wanted a government contract to financially sustain my speaking business. I prepared Requests for Proposals (RFPs) for almost a year. I thought there would be no end to all the paperwork and RRAs (Really Ridiculous Acronyms). After I submitted the proposals, months passed without a reply. I prayed, hoped, and waited, seemingly without an answer.

Finally, I called the office of one of the agencies and was told that they had decided not to do the programs. Then I received a letter indicating they had chosen someone else. Then I got an inquiry indicating they were resubmitting my request. I became disappointed and disillusioned with the governmental process. (Did I hear some "Amens"?) I wondered if the Good Shepherd had gone on vacation and left his sheep to wander—and wonder.

In retrospect now I see that the time I spent on the proposals and waiting for an answer was preparation for me to handle what God already had planned. You see, during the proposal writing time, I had to do a lot of research, compile a lot of training information, and do a lot of preparation that would never have occurred otherwise.

Finally, when God knew I was prepared to accept the challenges of my wants, he opened a door of opportunity and gave me a bigger and better contract with a private corporation that started an avalanche of new business in teaching cultural diversity. As the word spread about the success of the training and the benefits to corporations and governmental agencies, I began to receive calls from around the United States. For more than a decade, work rolled in. All the preparation paid off.

When I say, "The Lord is my Shepherd, I shall not be in want," it's more than just something to recite before eating. It's an affirmation that the Good Shepherd is watching over all the affairs of my life and is making sure I'm taken care of.

Have you been disappointed or disillusioned about something you wanted that God provided in a different way than you asked? Are you still waiting to hear a word from the Good

Shepherd? (Which is a whole lot better than waiting for word from the government.) The next time you hear this verse, concentrate on the assurance that you can depend on him to watch over you, to protect you, to provide for you, to comfort you, to chastise you when you need it, to bandage your wounds, to calm your fears, to care for your relationships, to communicate with you, and to love you unconditionally. You shall not be in want.

"Thank you, Lord, for reassuring us that your powerful, providing hand will be extended to us in life's situations. Please help us not to take you for granted. We praise you as the Shepherd of our lives. Amen."

START DREAMING

Luci Swindoll

However, as it is written: "No eye has seen,
no ear has heard, no mind has conceived
what God has prepared for those who love him"
—but God has revealed it to us by his Spirit.

1 CORINTHIANS 2:9–10

Vision is when you see it and others don't. Faith is when you do it and others won't.

My friend Joanne had both. A superb interior designer, she could see a finished room in her mind's eye and know how to transform the image into reality.

My brother Chuck has both. Although he stuttered as a child, he envisioned himself speaking publicly. With the help of a drama coach, he memorized poetry to quit stuttering. It solved the problem.

My hairdresser Gloria has both. Discouraged by the absence of her husband, who worked in another city, she quit a more lucrative job, moved to where he was, and opened her own beauty supply store.

With vision and faith things can be done. There's a couplet by Goethe, which reads:

Whatever you can do, or dream you can, begin it.
Boldness has genius, power, and magic in it.

I well remember the months I debated about buying my home. There I was, sixty-two years old, never having owned property, taking out a thirty-year loan. Was I crazy? I wanted a spot to call my own. I imagined what it would be like, and with God as my partner, I stepped out in faith. With confidence in his leading, I boldly went forward. It seemed like magic. And now, what joy this place brings me!

One of the greatest by-products of believing in something and then going for it is joy. I've often said, "My favorite thing in life is doing something new while having a good time." That's the essence of joy. Webster defines it as "a very glad feeling; great pleasure; delight."

The psalmist says, "Delight yourself in the LORD and he will give you the desires of your heart" (Psalm 37:4). I believe this works two ways. We delight, or find joy, in the Lord, and he gives us our heart's desires. He puts his desires in our hearts and then fulfills them. I like that. No, I delight in that.

Let's get practical. Perhaps you have an idea of something you would like to do, but you're scared. You've never done anything like it before. Maybe the idea just won't go away. But it's outside your comfort zone, and you don't feel adequate for the task. Start to pray, "Lord, if this desire is from you, will you bring it to pass? Help me know where to start."

And then start. This is the faith part. Work hard. Do what makes sense to you. And then do the next thing. Ask the Lord whom to talk to who might help you. Talk with them. Ask him to keep discouragement from your door.

As you go, you'll begin to experience boldness because you started. You acted on your desire. You saw it in your mind and you began.

That is exactly how I started to write thirteen years ago. Someone challenged me to write a book, and I was scared to death. But God gave me the desire, he answered when I prayed, and it was a delight.

What has he given you the desire to do? You can do it. Conceive the idea and trust him. Then start. And, with delight, see what happens!

"Give me your courage, Lord Jesus, to begin new things. Help me know what you want me to do, then enable me to do it joyfully. Amen."

PROMPTED

Patsy Clairmont

It is good to praise the LORD and make music
to your name, O Most High, to proclaim your love
in the morning and your faithfulness at night....
For you make me glad by your deeds, O LORD; I sing
for joy at the works of your hands. How great are your
works, O LORD, how profound are your thoughts!

PSALM 92:1–2, 4–5

I can remember the days when I bounded from bed in the morning, motor revving, ready to face the world. Well, okay, maybe I never truly bounded in the morning, but I know I had more days in which I hit the highway hollerin' than I have now. Today sludge moves faster than I do.

And moan ... oh, my, you should hear the series of groans that escape my lips as I force my frame into an upright position. The first couple of steps I attempt, boy, are they doozies, full of verbal rumblings. My body's soundtrack combines the creaks of an ancient door with the travailing of a birthing basset hound. Somehow, making these painful proclamations to express my physical struggle helps me trudge forward. I'm like an unoiled machine, an unprimed pump, and an unchained melody (that means I'm four notes short of a tune). I definitely need daybreak prompting.

I must admit the mirror is not the prompting monitor I had in mind. By the time I drag my weary body to the bathroom to face my reflection, it is a tad off-putting, to say the least. Though my bed-head does add humor, doesn't yours? Hair skittering in all directions with occasional wads spewing up like oil wells and knotted clumps secured to the scalp. It makes one wonder what one must have been dreaming about to cause such turbulence.

Here's the good news. We can only get better looking now that we're up. A good brushing, curling, back combing, spraying, and our hair begins to make sense—like it's supposed to be attached to our heads. Once we've adorned our frames with fashions, shod our feet with footwear, and covered our ... our ... our crevices with makeup, we are ready for a new day.

Actually, I need this rigorous (yes, for me this is rigorous) morning regimen to thoroughly wake me up. It shakes out the kinks in my body, dislodges the corrosion from my brain cells, and reactivates my lethargic will ... kinda.

"Imagine, Lord, that we would be reluctant to enter into a new day that you have carefully designed. Forgive our lagging bodies for not skipping in anticipation of your profound plans. Even when our bones lack their original suppleness, may our spirits be flexible so we can joyously stretch to meet with you. Our bodies may be slowing; yet, Lord, may our interior world be growing.

"We are grateful our good looks are not dependent on our disintegrating appearance. Lasting beauty emanates from you, Christ. You are our inner loveliness.

"For your beauty spills out a covering of grace allowing even the weariest, eldest, and crinkliest of your children (like me) to look her best.

"May your Holy Spirit be our daily prompter, and may we be your pleasing responders. May our wretched morning rumblings and grumblings turn to peals of praises and prayers. Amen."

REFUEL US AGAIN

Sheila Walsh

But Jesus often withdrew
to lonely places and prayed.

LUKE 5:16

Quiet places can be found in the noisiest spots, if you have the ears to hear them. I discovered that with a cat in my lap, a bird on my head, and a rabbit at my feet.

I was in my first year of theology graduate studies, and one of the classes I chose was "Foundations for Spiritual Life." At the end of the semester, part of the grade depended on taking a silent retreat at a monastery. The idea of silence was intriguing. I thought back to my days at Heathfield Primary School and how often I had to stand in the corner for talking too much.

Brother Michael greeted us students the day of our retreat. He invited us to spend the day enjoying God's presence on the monastery grounds. We agreed to meet up again later in the chapel, but until then we had several hours to ourselves. We all headed off in various directions.

I found a wonderful spot in the shade of an old tree. I sat for a few moments and enjoyed the scenery. It was a beautiful, clear day, and I could see for miles. I had a journal with me so I could write down whatever came to mind as I fellowshiped with God. I had my Bible and *Streams in the Desert*, my favorite devotional. I opened it to the reading for that day.

Halfway through the reading, a rabbit bounded across the path in front of me, and I stopped to watch its ears twitch as it sensed it wasn't alone. With a quick flip of its back legs it was gone.

I turned back to my book. In the distance I could hear a lone bird singing. Its whistle was plaintive and melodic. I listened for a while.

Then a large ginger cat parted a bush and walked across to where I was sitting with my back to the trunk of the tree. I scratched her ear, and she purred gratefully, settling down on my lap. I tried to read over her head, but she kept pushing the book out of the way to give me a better opportunity to scratch her ears.

This is no good, I thought. *I'm supposed to be meeting with God, not scratching a cat's ears. Sorry, Ginger, you're ruining the moment.*

I stood up and Ginger jumped to the ground, giving me a very disappointed look. She sauntered off. I walked a few paces deeper into the garden and came across a collection of gravestones. I knelt down to read the inscriptions and realized that each one spoke of a brother from the monastery who had died while serving there. The inscriptions were touching. These men obviously were loved and missed. I stood up and stretched and headed back to my tree.

I looked at my watch and saw that two hours had gone by, and I hadn't been very spiritual. I had all sorts of plans of what I would accomplish that day and definite expectations of what the day would look like, yet it wasn't working out that way.

You're a control freak, Sheila, I thought. *Let it go*.

I put down my books and journal and sat back against the tree. For the rest of the day, I just sat there. I didn't try to think holy thoughts or force my mind into a preconceived frame. I sat there with the rabbits and the birds and Ginger, who decided to give me a second chance.

It was a wonderful day. I found that as the sun began to set I had a deepened appreciation for the gift of solitude and for my sense of companionship with Christ as I sat surrounded by the wonder of his creation.

Holy moments come to us daily if we will ask for eyes to see. It may be the sun streaming through the window as you fold laundry. Or maybe it's lifting your friends to God while you vacuum. We can't always withdraw to quiet hillsides to pray, but Christ will meet with us in the quiet places of our hearts.

"In the stillness I worship you, God of all glory.
In the quiet I sing to you, Lord of all life.
Amen."

A QUIET LIFE

Luci Swindoll

[Pray] that we may lead a tranquil and quiet life
in all godliness and dignity.

I Timothy 2:2 NASB

I have a little plaque on my wall that reads, "Anything for a quiet life." I saw a bumper sticker today that suggested, "Honk if you love peace and quiet." I honked. I recently bought *The Little Book of Calm*. You get the picture. *Quiet, peace, calm*—even the words soothe my soul. That's why I love living in the desert.

The desert is a quiet place. Nobody hurries. My first week here I went to the grocery store, and right in the middle of the parking lot were two women, talking up a storm. Needing to park, I lightly beeped my horn and gestured for them to move to one side. Thinking I was waving, they simply smiled, waved back, and went right on talking. It didn't occur to them I would interrupt their conversation.

I love the community in the desert. Pat lives on my street, Patsy's a block away, and Marilyn, two. We take time to see each other, to have quiet time together, ignoring the hustle and bustle of life. I go by Marilyn's on my morning bike ride and drop off the newspaper. She offers me tea. We enjoy the visit. Pat and I go to our favorite place for lunch, just to talk. Patsy saunters by my house to compare notes on the book we're reading. My soul thrives here.

Just a couple of nights ago, an enormous, full moon appeared, and Mar and I sat on her back patio talking about prayer. We were there more than an hour. We didn't necessarily have the time; we chose to take it. When I got there, we both insisted we had only a few minutes. But neither of us wanted it to end.

The desert reminds me of my childhood in Texas: flat and dusty, with a big sky, frogs croaking, and crickets chirping. I take time to listen, and it's comforting. On hot summer evenings, I take a bubble bath and soak for a while, just to relax. I play beautiful music and sip a glass of cold lemonade.

But, when I want to completely retreat to the quiet life, it's not with my friends, the crickets, or the bath. It's with the Lord. Talk about a balm to my spirit. The joy and pleasure of speaking with the Lord is far superior to anything life on this earth affords. Through prayer I become centered and serene. When it's quiet and still, I sense the Lord comes near as I enter his presence.

I experience a silent symmetry when I'm alone with him that makes me calm. It strengthens me for the task at hand. In a culture where we all but worship activity and accomplishment, we can so easily miss time alone with him.

Remember what he said to Martha, who was such a little busy beaver, living, I guess, a loud and active life. He said, "Martha, Martha . . . you are worried and upset about many things, but only one thing is needed. Mary has chosen what is better" (Luke 10:41–42). We know what Mary was doing: sitting calmly, quietly, at the Master's feet.

When you're tempted to run around and never stop, let me challenge you. Choose the better part. Be with your friends, relax a little, and most necessarily, be with the Savior for a while. Ahh! Anything for a quiet life.

"Father, give me the courage to stop occasionally and the grace to take time for necessary things. Amen."

LISTEN AND LOVE

Barbara Johnson

You are my fortress, my refuge in times of trouble.

PSALM 59:16

The radio show was almost over. For nearly two hours I had sat beside the show's host, enjoying the interview and answering callers' comments and questions as best I could. Now I watched the clock behind his head, eagerly looking forward to the end of the show when I could take off my headset and say good-bye.

With about ten minutes to go, the host took a call from a trembly-voiced woman who had just discovered her son was a homosexual. "Barbara, I believe homosexuality is wrong, and I want to help my son, to show him how far he's strayed. But he won't listen to me. He says he won't even come home anymore if I'm going to 'preach' at him. I just don't know what to do!"

I glanced at the host as the caller's voice broke. His eyes were closed, and his face wore a painful grimace, as though the woman's words had somehow given him a sudden headache.

"Well, I can certainly tell you what not to do," I told the caller. "Don't preach at him, don't quote Bible verses at him, and don't recite any spiritual laws. That's what I learned through painful experience when I found out my own son was involved in homosexuality. The words I said drove him away from me for eleven years. I tell parents to put a sock in their mouths and listen when their child comes home. Just listen and love. Those are the two best things you can do. One way to show your love is to listen. As someone said, to *lessen* a person's pain, *listen* with your heart."

By now all the color had drained from the host's face. *Poor thing. He must have a migraine*, I thought as I continued with my response to the caller.

"Let me tell you what Billy Graham said about this. When he was on *20/20* recently, Hugh Downs asked Billy whether, if he had a gay son, he could still love that son. Billy didn't hesitate. He said, 'Oh, I'd love that son more!' He knew that child would need more love, and that would be the only way he could ever reach out to him."

As the caller hung up, the host, now looking as if he were about to cry, flipped off the microphone. The program broke for a commercial. "Barb," he said, "could you please finish up the show alone? I . . . I have to step outside a minute."

Thunderstruck, I stuttered, "B-b-by myself . . . ?" But he was already gone. Before I could even catch my breath, the technician was pointing to me through the window of the control room and making a rolling motion with her finger. Through the headset I heard, "Barb, you're on the air."

I managed to press the blinking buttons on the telephone for a couple of more calls, and then, thankfully, the show ended. As I took off my headset and leaned back in the chair, the host returned to the studio.

"I'm so sorry to do that to you, Barb, but I just couldn't go on," he said. "I've been in broadcasting for twenty-five years, and I thought I could handle anything that came my way, but what you said to that caller gripped me like nothing has before. You see . . ." He paused for a moment, struggling to stay in control. "Our son just told us he's gay. My wife came completely unglued."

My heart ached for the man, knowing exactly how he felt. He was stuck in one of life's potholes, and it felt like a parade of tractortrailers was rumbling over his battered body.

A parent's life is hard. Just as you're sighing with relief after getting the kid through diapers, daycare, driving, and diplomas, along comes a genuine disaster that makes you long for the days when your biggest dilemma was preparing enough formula or getting all the diapers laundered. When these life storms smash us on the ceiling, the only thing we can do is love—love God and love our children, and turn them over to the Lord to fix. Proverbs 10:12 reminds us, "Love covers over all wrongs," and that's true for *all* of God's children.

How wonderful for us hurting parents that we don't have to endure life's tragedies alone. Our loving heavenly Father is with us when our children break our hearts. Clinging to God's Word, we keep breathing and keep believing. As the psalmist wrote, "My comfort in my suffering is this: Your promise preserves my life" (Psalm 119:50).

"Dear Lord, you are my strength and my comforter. I cling to you when life-storms threaten to destroy me. Thank you, Father, for clinging back! Amen."

SLEEPLESS IN ETERNITY

Marilyn Meberg

He will never let me stumble, slip or fall.
For he is always watching, never sleeping.

PSALM 121:3–4 TLB

I resent the need for sleep. I can't remember a time in my life when the call to sleep was appealing. In fact, not only is sleep unappealing, it's boring. For example, I awakened about 3:15 this morning and was stunned at the amount of intense light streaming through my slightly parted vertical blinds.

I thought, *There's a searchlight beaming in on the condo. I'm going to be apprehended for something. Now there's a touch of drama for such an early hour!*

Peeking through the verticals, I realized a brilliant full moon was responsible for all that brightness. No SWAT team, no foreign agents, just an incredible moon.

I wanted to grab a jacket, hop on my bike, and ride around the neighborhood. That moon was simply going to waste out there. But did I dare? Of course not! For one thing, a widow peddling about at 3:15 in the morning with traces of sleep garment trailing beneath her jacket might communicate a questionable message. Not only that—and here's where I get really resentful—if I were to cavort about in the moonlight, I'd feel rotten the next day. Why? Because sleep is mandatory; without it we're groggy and tired.

Wouldn't it be fun if sleep were voluntary? Sleep if you feel like it, don't if you don't feel like it.

My favorite city is New York. You've probably heard it described as the city that never sleeps. Well, that's what I love about it. Everyone appears to consider sleep a voluntary activity. People are on the sidewalks all night long. If I should take to the streets in New York at 3:15 in the morning, no one would think a thing of it.

The Hephzibah House is my favorite place to stay in New York. It's an old brownstone Christian guest house just down a half block from Central Park and about three blocks from Lincoln Center—a wonderful neighborhood. During one of my stays there, my good friend Mary Graham and I decided to stroll through the streets before settling down for the night. Though it was midnight in New York, it was only nine o'clock on the West Coast, and I was eager to walk my airplane-cramped legs. A gently falling snow thrilled me as I snuggled deeply into my goose down coat. I was suffused with contentment.

"Mary," I said, "do you think the need for sleep is part of the fallout from the Fall in the Garden of Eden? Do you think I can pin that one on Adam and Eve?"

We kicked the idea around for awhile. The first couple ate food before the Fall; was that voluntary or was it a need? If one were living in a perfect place like Eden, we agreed that probably there were no needs, just delicious choices. Food for them might simply have been a delicious choice; so might sleep.

We stepped into an all-night (of course) little diner, and while sipping our respective cups of herbal tea, I began to feel sleepy. The diner was full of people talking animatedly, some slurping hot beverages, others eating bacon and eggs. Outside I could see the snow still falling, and the sidewalks filled with people moving about.

"Mary," I said, "Adam and Eve really tick me off. Sleep is not a delicious choice for me. It's a need. That need is their fault!"

Smiling wearily she said, "Yeah, they tick me off too," and with that we made our way back to the Hephzibah House.

Two thoughts comfort me about God and the whole sleep thing. When Scripture states that he watches over us and will not slumber, I'm thrilled to realize that should I wake up in the night, he's awake too. I hate being the only one awake in the night. Some of my best times with him have occurred during the wee hours of the morning when no one else is alert. I've settled enormous issues during some of those nocturnal chats. Other times I've just felt comforted by his presence. Sometimes there's no talk at all. I just know he's there.

The other comfort is that because God does not sleep, and because Scripture says in heaven I shall be like him, the day is coming when I, too, won't have to sleep! That means in eternity, where there is no night, I can read endlessly, chat interminably, or even sing endlessly. I won't grow tired, and I won't get sleepy. That heavenly prospect floods me with joy as well as anticipation. What a reward for going to bed on earth!

I guess until that eternity comes, I'll quit griping about Adam and Eve. Then again, maybe I won't; they still tick me off.

"Lord, thank you that even in the wee hours of the morning you are there watching over me. You're there to listen, to comfort, to encourage, and to enlighten. You're there to just be there; thank you for that. Amen."

TICKED

Patsy Clairmont

The wise heart will know the proper time.

ECCLESIASTES 8:5

Remember the Tidy Bowl Man? Well, I think his brother lives in my clock! Honest, someone is in my clock trying to get out. I can hear him tapping. If I knew Morse code, maybe I could decipher his little pleas for help. Day and night, more on than off, tap, tap, tap. Since it's a clock radio, maybe the tapping is actually the Tidy Bowl Brother (T.B.B.) dancing. Maybe his taps are raps. Perhaps this is Radio Rapper. Then again, T.B.B. may just be fed up with being trapped by time and wants someone to heed his frustration.

We all seem to live by the ever-tapping clock. Frequently, when I ask a friend to join me for tea, I hear, "I wish I could, but I have to make it to ___________." Fill in the blank with "my appointment," "my plane," "my deadline." We huff and puff through our hours wondering where, oh where, the day has gone. Perplexing, isn't it, how little and at times how much can be accomplished with the moments we've been given?

I'm usually running behind, playing catch up, and robbing Petula to pay Paulette. Yet give me a day off, and it slips through my fingers (like my last paycheck). Then, the harder I try to hang on to special moments, the faster the clock seems to tick. Which ticks me off because the hard days, the painful days, the boring days, seem to contain endless hours.

All told, at the age of fifty-two, my years have been as the Scripture said they would be, "like a vapor." Poof! Fifty-two years have come and gone.

At the close of a day, I always mentally run back through my accomplishments or lack thereof. The thereofs are the aggravating tap, tap, tapping reminders and rap, rap, rapping regrets about what I didn't do or should have done. You know what? I think the Tidy Bowl Brother and I might be kindred spirits. I, too, feel encased within a timepiece that can at times rob me of my peace. Instead of tapping or rapping, my way of dealing with the ever-present clock is flapping. I spread my stubby wings and try to lift my chubby frame off the ticking tarmac only to crash-land like one of those gooney birds who flails beak-first into the earth.

Earth is the problem, you know. As long as we remain bound to the earth in this life, we will be restricted by an ever-present ticking-tapping clock. When the day comes that we are freed from time and enter our sweet liberty, we will never again have to consult a Big Ben or a Bulova. Hallelujah! Until then, we need to make peace with the timepiece so we, unlike the T.B.B., don't spend our time beating our heads against the clock. Here are some tips. I'll try them if you will.

1. Don't cram every day so full you can't enjoy the journey.
2. Don't underplan and miss the thrill of a fruitful day.
3. Don't underestimate a nap, a rocking chair, and a good book.
4. Don't become a sloth.
5. Do offer your gratitude for the moments assigned to you.
6. Do celebrate even the passing of days. (For he designed it thus—poof!)
7. Do enter into your time here on earth not flapping but soaring. Ride out your days with a sense of your limitless future in a timeless eternity.

"Lord, thank you for the structure of time so we don't flit or flap away our days. Help us to rest and to run in right proportions. For left unto ourselves, some of us would race and others of us would rust. Either way we would speed past or sleep through the joy. Teach us, Lord, to value our days and redeem our moments. In Jesus' everlasting name. Amen."

NAME DROPPERS

Barbara Johnson

Our help is in the name of the LORD,
the Maker of heaven and earth.

PSALM 124:8

At the call center in Denver International Airport, each of the thirty-six operators may answer as many as 260 calls per day. Then they relay messages to some of the ninety thousand passengers and others who pass through the concourses within any twenty-four-hour period.

Sometimes the messages are frantic, such as one from a daughter who helped her father carry his luggage to the check-in counter for his trip to Bangkok and then returned to the parking lot to discover a major problem. That's when the call center might relay a message begging, "Don't get on that plane! You have Sarah's only set of car keys in your pocket."

I read about one man who called his wife from an airport pay phone. When he had used up all his coins, the operator interrupted to say he had one minute left. The man hurriedly tried to finish his conversation with his wife, but before they could tell each other good-bye, the line went dead. With a sigh, the man hung up the phone and started to leave the little telephone cubicle. Just then the phone rang. Thinking it was the operator wanting more money, the man almost didn't answer. But something told him to pick up the phone. And sure enough, it was the operator. But she didn't want more money. Instead, she had a message for him.

"After you hung up, your wife said she loved you," the operator said. "I thought you'd want to know."

Similar tender-hearted operators were described in Michael Booth's article in the *Denver Post* (July 11, 1997). The article portrayed the hectic pace of a day in Denver's airport call center. One supervisor said he sometimes relays messages from lovesick girlfriends who beg him to page their traveling boyfriends. "So the guy hears his page and calls in, and I say, 'Sally says she loves you,' and he's standing there [wondering], 'How do *you* know?'" the supervisor said.

Sometimes the names to be paged are so difficult to pronounce the operators have to connect to a "language line" that helps them translate different dialects. Then there's the Forbidden Name List, a computer compilation of names with hidden meanings that the operators are instructed not to broadcast. For example, you will not hear this page at the Denver airport: "Ms. Bath, Ms. Anita Bath." Nor will you hear, "Mr. Dover, Mr. Ben Dover" or "Ms. Popp, Ms. Lolly Popp."

Sometimes, though, a caller slips one over on the wary operators. That happened last summer, when a page rang out through the airport for "Mr. Dopolina, Mr. Bob Dopolina." Then, according to the *Post*, "thousands of passengers could sing along with the rest of the tune, 'Bobdopolina-da-bop-bam-boom!'"

When I read about these relayed messages, I chuckled, but then I thought of how fortunate we are that when we need to get an urgent message to our Father in heaven, we don't have to route our plea through a busy call center. Isaiah 58:9 promises, "Then you will call, and the LORD will answer."

We don't have to worry that he'll think we're a fictitious person. He has known us—each one of us—since he knit us together in our mothers' wombs (Psalm 139:13).

He knows us by name (Exodus 33:17), and he'll never stumble over the pronunciation or forget who we are. He wears our names on his hands (Isaiah 49:16).

And we can be assured that he knows more than just our names; he knows all about us (Psalm 139:3)—and loves us anyway! It's not a situation like the one in which a little boy ran to the sidelines and told his mother after tryouts for the soccer team, "Mom, I guess I'm better than I thought; the coaches must have heard of me. They just called everyone else by his number, but they kept calling me by name!"

His mother didn't have the heart to point out to him that he was the only one with his name imprinted above the number on the back of his shirt.

"Dear God, you whisper my name, and my fears subside. You carve my name on your hand, and I delight in knowing I'm there. You read my innermost thoughts—the pain I bear, the stress I endure, the joy I seek, and the love I have for you—and you understand. Thank you, Lord! Amen."

DADDY

Marilyn Meberg

"I will be a Father to you, and you will be my sons and daughters," says the Lord Almighty.

2 CORINTHIANS 6:18

Certain animals always make me giggle. The more peculiar they look, the more awkwardly they move, the more off-the-wall their habits, the more they amuse me. This summer I had occasion to be in London and was contentedly perusing *The London Times* one morning while drinking a cup of brisk English tea. As I flipped over to page four, to my utter delight the newspaper showed a huge picture of a baby ostrich. This baby was in the act of running as fast as its spindly little legs would carry him. Ostriches rank among the highest giggle-producers for me, and so I dove into the story with high expectations.

Instead of finding the story funny, I found it charmingly poignant. A gentleman who owns the zoo in Welland, Worcestershire, faced a dilemma. He needed a father ostrich for four recently hatched babies. As soon as chicks are hatched in the wild, the father runs off at top speed followed by his brood. This develops the leg muscles, which ultimately enable the ostrich to run up to forty miles per hour.

However, these little chicks were not born in the wild but in the zoo. So the zoo's owner was advertising for volunteers to impersonate a male ostrich for two hours a day. The volunteer must be able to run twenty miles per hour and flap his arms like wings at the same time. The owner of the zoo said the person needed to be fit because, if you stop running, the baby sits down.

"A top athlete would be ideal for this job," the gentleman said, "but any fit individual who doesn't mind flapping and running at the same time would be great. The chicks think you're their father. They have good eyesight, but they aren't very clever."

I was amused at the thought of volunteering to impersonate a male ostrich, but I found myself more caught up with the need of the babies to have a father who would teach them what they must know to survive in the world.

In contrast to the gentle poignancy of that story is the account I read last week about juvenile delinquent elephants who are killing rhinos in Pilanesberg National Park in northwestern South Africa by kneeling on them and then goring them. The youthful elephants have no motive for killing other than what appears to be the pleasure of it.

Game wardens and animal behavior experts have a theory, and while they stress that it's speculative, the idea is arresting. The troublemaker elephants are all orphans, taken as calves from their parents during cutting operations in the Kruger National Park. The babies were relocated to establish elephant populations in parks and private reserves throughout South Africa.

Most of the relocated calves were males and were raised with no exposure to adult elephants or the hierarchical social structure that defines elephant life. The long-term effect of this isolation appears to be a generation of juvenile delinquents. Under normal circumstances a dominant older male elephant keeps young bulls in line. For the newly relocated elephants, no such role models exist. Early next year, a few forty-year-old bull elephants will be moved to Pilanesberg to help calm things down.

The parallel between the fatherless elephants in need of a strong male role model and our own human societal structure is striking. We know juvenile crime is highest among those who come from broken homes without fathers.

Isn't it interesting that the divine imprint for order in our world is evidenced in all of creation, both animal and human? God created the male to perform a God-inspired role. When that role is disrupted, abandoned, or aborted, disorder and chaos often result. Of course at times a father's absence doesn't bring disorder as much as it brings a deep sense of loss in male modeling.

Ken's father died when Ken was twelve, and he retained wonderful memories of his dad's commitment to Christ and family. Even so, there was a hole in Ken's soul that could never be filled. He wanted and needed a dad to guide him through his teenage years, the choosing of a career, and the development of his theology of living. In spite of a loving mother, at times he needed a dad.

One of the most touching Scriptures is Galatians 4:6 in which God says to us, "Because you are sons, God sent the Spirit of his Son into our hearts, the Spirit who calls out '*Abba*, Father.'" The Hebrew word *abba* means "daddy." We are reminded that we are never totally fatherless, and in times of quiet despair, we can cry out a prayer like this:

"Daddy, oh Daddy, comfort me, hold me. I so need your touch. I so need your tender presence. Be with me, dear Daddy. Let me rest in you, relax in you, and find peace in you. Amen."

CLOSET LIVING

Barbara Johnson

Praise be to . . . the Father of compassion
and the God of all comfort, who comforts us in all
our troubles, so that we can comfort those in any trouble
with the comfort we ourselves have received from God.

2 CORINTHIANS 1:3–4

The woman's letter was four sheets of stationery covered front and back with tiny, neat handwriting. Her words poured out her anguish over her husband's infidelity, her own devastating health problems, and finally, their child's announcement that he was a homosexual. At the top of the first page she had printed in big, boxy letters: "Barb, please do not print any of this, as I'm still in the closet."

Hurting parents all over the world are huddled right now in a million mental closets of dark despair. One woman wrote a letter that said, "My gay son came out of the closet, Barb, and we went in!" Another said, "After our son told us he was gay, we landed on the ceiling, just like you did, Barb. Then we fell flat on the floor and tumbled right into the closet. It's been almost a year, and we're still there."

To paraphrase Art Linkletter, kids say the awfulest things. And one of the hardest things to hear is, "Mom and Dad, I'm gay." That's when so many Christian parents, their hearts broken, their stomachs tied in knots, and their egos shattered by humiliation, find themselves locked in the closet, barely able to breathe let alone function normally.

If you're a parent in pain, here's some good news: You're not in that closet alone. Jesus said, "Lo, I am with you always, even in the farthest corner of the darkest closet" (Hurting Parents' translation of Matthew 28:20). Quiet your sobbing for a moment and sense his presence there beside you. Feel yourself welcomed into his arms, pressed against his heart, filled with his love and tender mercy, comforted by his promises. He knows how you hurt. After all, he loves your wayward child even more than you do!

Finally, when you find yourself empowered with the tiniest morsel of strength, let go with one hand and reach out to another hurting parent huddled in the darkness of the closet. As someone said, God didn't put us on this earth to be the comforted but to be the comforters. The prophet Isaiah wrote, "The LORD has anointed Me . . . to heal the brokenhearted, . . . to comfort all who mourn" (Isaiah 61:1b–2 NKJV).

If you're a parent, pain is inevitable, but misery is optional. Just because you're feeling down, don't think your world is ending. As the saying goes, even the sun has a sinking spell every evening. But the next morning, like bread dough in the darkness of the oven, it rises.

We Christian parents can hit bottom just like anyone else. But we have a special ability that nonbelievers don't have. We bounce! So when you feel yourself plummeting into that closet, be sure to leave the door open. That way you won't knock it down on your way out.

"Heavenly Father, be with me in the closet. Amen."

COMING HOME

Sheila Walsh

If we confess our sins, he is faithful and just and will forgive us our sins and purify us from all unrighteousness.

1 John 1:9

I love homecomings. That's one of the reasons I treasure every opportunity I have to take a trip back to my native Scotland. On one such trip I was a guest singer at a Billy Graham crusade. I sat with the rain bouncing off the platform as George Beverly Shea sang the lovely hymn,

> *"Softly and tenderly Jesus is calling,*
> *calling for you and for me."*

I looked out at the crowd gathered in a Scottish soccer stadium on that soggy Saturday afternoon and marveled that Dr. Billy Graham could fill the place. If it had been Chicago or New York, I would have expected a vast sea of faces, but there, on my own home ground, I was overwhelmed. I watched the crowd hanging on every word.

> *"Come home, come home*
> *All who are weary come home."*

Billy's message was simple and uncompromising. No bells or whistles "wowed" the crowd, just a simple call was made to "Come home." I looked out at shaved heads and tattoos, children running through puddles, and wrinkled, weary old faces huddling under umbrellas, and I wondered what the response would be.

I wondered if the message sounded too good to be true. I wondered if it sounded too simple.

But then it began . . . Like a waterfall, people began to stream to the front to receive Christ. I had to bury my face in my hands, overwhelmed with pure joy at being a spectator to such a homecoming. I thought of the Scripture, "I tell you that in the same way there will be more rejoicing in heaven over one sinner who repents than over ninety-nine righteous persons who do not need to repent" (Luke 15:7). I knew a big homecoming celebration was going on in heaven right then.

When the crusade was over, I was waiting at the side of the stage for my ride back to the hotel. A woman wrapped up in a plaid raincoat touched my arm. "I enjoyed hearing you sing tonight," she said.

"Thanks!" I replied. "Wasn't it a wonderful evening!"

"It was for me," she said. "I'll never be the same again."

"What do you mean?" I asked.

She stopped and looked at me for a moment as if struggling to put it into words. "I've gone to church all my life, but tonight, I came home."

I put my arms round her and hugged her, and the tears and the rain ran rivers down our faces.

I wonder if, like this woman, you've been circling the building for years but never come home? It would be such a shame to sit in church every Sunday and listen to what's being said about God but never grasp that this is a personal invitation, a homecoming, a welcome mat thrown on the ground just for you.

"If we confess our sins, he is faithful and just and will forgive us our sins and purify us from all unrighteousness" (1 John 1:9). Isn't that great? Isn't that simple? All you have to do is pray.

"Father, thank you that you love me. Thank you that Jesus died for me. I want to come home. Thank you for waiting for me. Amen."

We Brake for Joy! is based on the popular Women of Faith conferences. Women of Faith is partnering with Zondervan Publishing House, Integrity Music, *Today's Christian Woman* magazine, and Campus Crusade to offer conferences, publications, worship music, and inspirational gifts that support and encourage today's Christian women.

Since their beginning in January of 1996, the Women of Faith conferences have enjoyed an enthusiastic welcome by women across the country. Women of Faith conference plans presently extend through the year 2000. Call 1-888-49-FAITH for the many conference locations and dates available.

See the following pages for additional information about Women of Faith products.

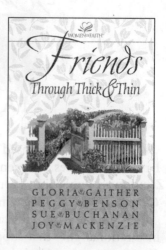

Deeper Joy for Your Journey

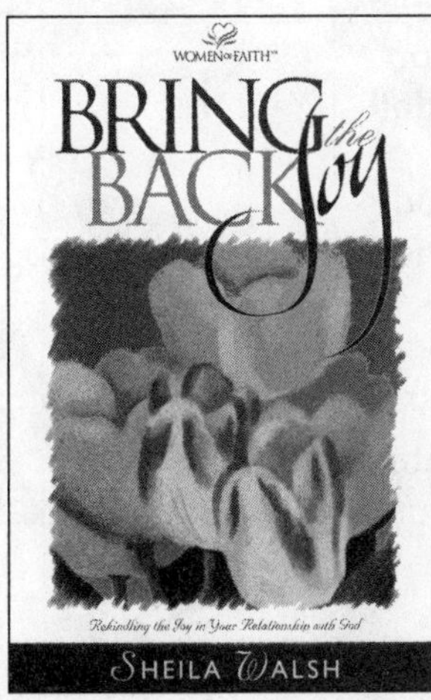

Bring Back the Joy

Sheila Walsh

Capturing the theme of the 1998 Women of Faith™ conferences, *Bring Back the Joy* is a warm, encouraging, and richly personal invitation to experience the joy that comes from loving and being loved by the Most Important Person in the Universe. In *Bring Back the Joy*, Sheila Walsh writes about rekindling the joy in your life and in your relationship with God. With great wisdom gained through learning and growing with other women as a key speaker at Women of Faith conferences across the nation, she calls us to a deeper joy, exposes the negative forces designed to steal our joy, and shows us how to sow life-changing seeds of joy.

Hardcover 0-310-22023-8
Audio Pages 0-310-22222-2

More for Your Joyful Journey . . .

The Joyful Journey

Patsy Clairmont, Barbara Johnson, Marilyn Meberg, and Luci Swindoll

With trademark warmth and good humor, the authors share from their hearts and lives about the obstacles, bumps, and detours we sometimes face along the journey of life and about how friendship, laughter, and celebration can help steer our hearts closer to God.

Softcover 0-310-22155-2
Audio Pages 0-310-21454-8

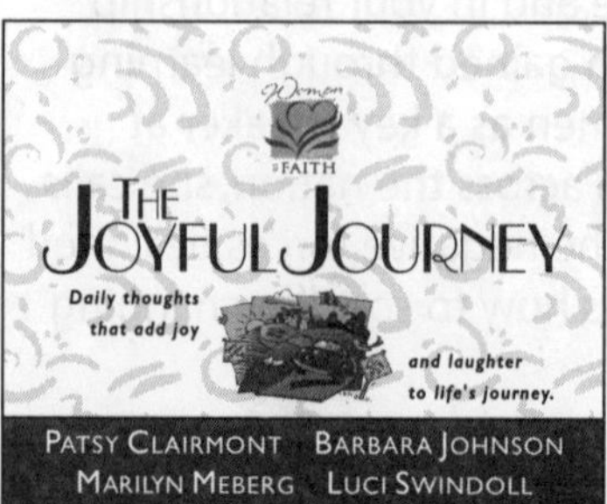

The Joyful Journey

Perpetual Calendar Daybreak

Three hundred sixty-six encouraging and inspiring excerpts from the book by Patsy Clairmont, Barbara Johnson, Marilyn Meberg, and Luci Swindoll celebrate life and bring joy and laughter every day of the year!

0-310-97282-5

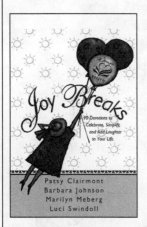

We want to hear from you. Please send your comments about this book to us in care of the address below. Thank you.

ZondervanPublishingHouse
Grand Rapids, Michigan 49530
http://www.zondervan.com